Searching for Creativity in the Chinese TEFL Context

中国环境下的创造性英语教学探索

段平华 著

吉林大学出版社

·长春·

图书在版编目（CIP）数据

中国环境下的创造性英语教学探索 / 段平华著. --长春：吉林大学出版社，2020.3
ISBN 978-7-5692-6178-3

Ⅰ.①中… Ⅱ.①段… Ⅲ.①英语-教学研究-高等学校 Ⅳ.①H319.3

中国版本图书馆 CIP 数据核字（2020）第 036563 号

书　　名	中国环境下的创造性英语教学探索 ZHONGGUO HUANJING XIA DE CHUANGZAOXING YINGYU JIAOXUE TANSUO
作　　者	段平华　著
策划编辑	李伟华
责任编辑	李卓彦
责任校对	刘　丹
装帧设计	王　艳
出版发行	吉林大学出版社
社　　址	长春市人民大街 4059 号
邮政编码	130021
发行电话	0431-89580028/29/21
网　　址	http://www.jlup.com.cn
电子邮箱	jdcbs@jlu.edu.cn
印　　刷	北京厚诚则铭印刷科技有限公司
开　　本	787mm×1092mm　　1/16
印　　张	13.25
字　　数	230 千字
版　　次	2021 年 3 月　第 1 版
印　　次	2021 年 3 月　第 1 次
书　　号	ISBN 978-7-5692-6178-3
定　　价	48.00 元

版权所有　翻印必究

序言 1

本书建立在中国英语专业师生对于创造力（CREATIVITY）的理解和概念的研究基础之上，通过深刻分析当前中国英语专业在英语教学中只注重英语语言本身的教学，忽视其信息的学习和学生创造力培养，以及中国整个外语语言教学"高耗低效"的现象，阐述了作者对于如何充分调动学生的学习积极性，培养学生的创造力和创造精神，同时大幅度提高英语教学效率的独到思考和见解。

本书的两大部分（SECTION A 和 SECTION B）既相互联系，又相对独立。从形式上看，第一部分（SECTION A）是一篇结构完整的大论文，第二部分（SECTION B）则是几篇各自相对独立的论文，是第一部分的延续和发展。

书的第一部分，作者在分析我国英语专业教学领域的现状和问题（Chapter One），总结国内外创造学方面前沿研究成果的基础上，对可能促进和阻碍中国学生创造力发展的各种因素进行了探讨，并提出了该论文的核心研究问题（Chapter Two）。作者用了整整一章的篇幅详细探讨了该课题所采用的定性研究方法：包括选用具体研究方法的理由，本课题研究模型的构建，具体实施细节和注意事项的描述，参与者的背景状况、数据处理和分析过程等，同时预期了本研究的局限性（Chapter Three）。在结果与讨论一章里（Chapter Four），作者将收集整理出来的数据进行了细致的分析，揭示了英语专业学生对于创造力的理解、可能存在的问题，以及对于我国英语教学，特别是英语专业教学的启示。最后，作者通过总结数据分析结果，回答了第一章提出的核心研究问题，客观地分析了研究的局限性，并对后续研究的可能性提出了建议（Chapter Five）。该论文写作形式完整规范、态度严谨、观点新颖、表达准确，是值得英语专业硕士研究生在撰写毕业论文前反复研读的，一篇不可多得的优秀范文。

在书的第二部分（SECTION B），作者对如何在英语专业教学过程中，打破学生传统封闭的习惯性思维方式，培养学生批判性思维和创新能力，同时大幅度提高其英语语言能力的理论和方法方面进行了探讨。首先（CHAPTER

ONE B），作者通过观察两位中国读者和两位英语国家的外国读者在阅读了同样一首英语诗后，分别进行的讨论和分析对话，探讨了在文学教学中，教师应该如何有效运用维果茨基（Vygotsky）的"最近发展区"理论，为中国学生搭建知识建构的"脚手架"，提供正确处理好传统教学法与自我反应理论和读者反应理论的关系的方法；作者提出，在鼓励学生大胆思考和想象，主动参与作品篇章处理过程的同时，还必须从中国学生的实际出发，及时检查、发现和纠正他们在理解英语原文过程中由于"语言硬壳效应"而出现的偏差，使他们的文学学习和创造性思维朝着正确的方向发展。在第五章（CHAPTER FIVE B），通过对于传统英语角兴衰史的分析，作者指出：由于传统的英语角组织形式松散等原因，没有旺盛的生命力作为基础，注定是虎头蛇尾的、失败的。与此同时，作者创造性地提出了英语日的初步设想，并描述了作者具体实施英语日的过程和效果。这一篇论文在1996年发表在《中国英语教学》杂志上之后，在各地引起了不同程度的反响，一时间，"英语日"在很多地方和单位开展了起来。第六章（CHAPTER SIX B）题为《英力克英语习得模式监控方式的研究》，是一个省级科研项目的结题报告英文版。通过一千多名外语系英语专业师生进行了两年的实验，经过定量和定性等实证性研究手段，说明了英力克英语习得模式假说的有效性和可行性，即语言不仅可以在母语国家通过自然习得的方式获得，也可以在非母语地区通过人为地创造相应的语言交际运用的自然习得环境，结合语言学习的方式获得，其语言能力获得的效率将大大高于单纯依赖课堂的学习方式；但这种人为外语语言环境只有通过建立合理的监控激励机制才能真正形成。研究还说明，通过一系列的英力克活动，特别是英语日活动，学生们的英语语言能力得到大幅度提高的同时，其自信心、综合素质和创新精神也得到了明显加强。这一实验为英力克习得模式的假设（ENLLIC Acquisition Hypothesis）建立了基础。

  本书作者段平华副教授对英语语言学的研究有较深的造诣，并在英语语言学教学实践中积累了丰富的经验。从字里行间，可以看出作者在捕捉选题方面的敏锐与独到、探讨和选择研究方法方面的深思熟虑、研究过程的精益求精、英语语言表达的准确流畅，堪称上乘的英语学术论文，是一本难得的好书。因此，本书既是高等院校英语专业教师进行专业教学研究与实践的引玉之砖，也是英语专业学生撰写英语毕业论文和课程论文的优秀参考范文。

  相信本书的出版，必将受到高等院校英语专业教师和学生的欢迎和青睐。

原一川（教授、博士）
2007年8月30日

Preface 2

If one had to identify the most important factor in the development EFL/ESL teaching theory and practice in China since the late 1970's or early 1980's it would have to be the communicative language teaching approach. However, with the rapid development of globalization and "opening up," English is being increasingly used as an international language. This implies a need to seriously rethink the traditional approaches to language teaching which often implied (for some people at least) an unrealistic goal of native "speakership" at the expense of real communication in the target language. Fortunately, the emphasis is now shifting toward the more pragmatic ideal in communicative competence whereby language is used to achieve some practical, functional purpose in daily life. The process of change is not easy and curriculum developers as well as teachers at all levels in the education system are constantly up against the entrenched values of older approaches.

It is against this background that Duan Ping-Hua's book: Seeking for Creativity in Chinese TEFL Contexts, has been written. This is a timely publication and has been written at a stage when English teachers, particularly at college and university level, are looking for new ways of challenging their EFL students to be more reflective about the way that language functions in an increasingly globalized world.

Section A of the book (TEFL and Beyond TEFL) which is a slightly remodelled version of the author's M. A. thesis, is a valuable contribution to the arguments for more creativity in EFL programs in Chinese college and university settings. The findings of the research study are interesting and show what some educational thinkers have long believed—that good language programs need a content base for flexible, creative outcomes. These outcome contrasts with the more traditional practice whereby the focus has tended to be given to the form of the language, leading to an observation that many English major graduates seem unable to effectively operate in real communication in the real world. Of course, one should not neglect the vital role of the teacher in all of this. The author is very mindful of this aspect and is careful to demonstrate, through his research findings, that some teachers' open-ended activities (along with content teaching) are positively related to the expression of students' creativity.

Section B, Theories and Practice: Exploring Creative TEFL Methodology in the Chinese Context continues the theme opened up in Section A, but at an applied level of actual teaching and interaction. In the first chapter of this section (Cultivating pluralistic thinking through literature teaching) the author notes that the literature of English is a most ideal course for students to "train and pluralize" their thinking. This is further reinforcement of the need for a content base for language development noted in Section A of the book. The author uses the model of Jane Eyre and Wide Sargasso Sea as an example to effectively demonstrate (through comparative method) how a carefully planned literature program can enliven thinking and stretch language resources to the limit as students struggle to give 'a voice' to their ideas.

Chapter Two in Section B (Maximizing the expertise of native English speaking teachers in China) is also particularly interesting and practical-especially for newly arrived foreign teachers. Such teachers are often puzzled about their expected roles and to whether or not they overstep these roles. It may come as a surprise for them to find that students might actually greatly appreciate the language opportunities that come about through less formal out-of-class contact. Other chapters in this section also provide useful insights for both Chinese and foreign teachers.

Overall, this is a valuable book. There are numerous ways that the potential reader could find benefit from it. As already noted in this Preface, the central theme is to recognize the fresh and challenging ideas that come out of thinking about the notion of creativity in language. Curriculum developers or teachers working on new programs for English majors might well find benefit from Section A of the book in particular. Another way of gaining benefit from the book is to engage with the challenge of planning English programs around content. This may be as simple as presenting extracts from, for instance, the *China Daily* newspaper (which often publishes interesting and challenging cartoons on contemporary issues in China). The aim would be to challenge thinking, to 'stretch' existing language-not simply to arrange for students to have a 'safe' discussion which may do very little for actual language development. The insights contained in several of the chapters in Section B, relating to cross-cultural and social factors in teaching and learning in Chinese colleges and universities, are enlightening and are worth a close study, particularly by foreigners planning to teach or work in China-or who are already in these roles.

I have great pleasure in recommending this book. I feel it has much to offer to people working-or thinking about working in Chinese educational settings. It was my privilege to have been associated with the author over several years, both as a supervisor of his M. A. thesis and also as a colleague.

Kevin J. Smith

Foreign Expert, Yunnan Normal University.
Former Senior Lecturer, LaTrobe University (Bendigo Campus), Australia

Preface 3

I have lived in China for fifteen years and have been a foreign English teacher for eleven of those. I have discovered one very slowly changing fact, creativity in a Chinese classroom setting is almost non-existent. But, most foreign-teacher-taught classrooms (that I have experienced in China) are founded on creativity and the encouragement of it. The above factor adds greatly to the already existing atmosphere of foreign teacher and Chinese student relational confusion.

The author of this book, Duan Pinghua, has made a wonderful effort toward helping us to understand some of the elements that create these relational problems Creativity and relationships between students and foreign teachers (in a Chinese setting), is one of the most misunderstood subjects in China's education system. As China's education system evolves and students continue to change their world views and goals, creativity in teaching and a greater understanding of student-teacher relationships must evolve with it.

Duan Pinghua has reminded us (with this volume) that creativity in the Chinese classroom setting will need to be encouraged and creativity in teaching methods will need to be implemented. He has reminded us that a far greater effort towards understanding student/teacher relationships must be a primary goal of administrators, teachers (foreign and Chinese) and students alike. This will be a crucial factor in training young minds for China's future.

We need more volumes like this one, by Duan Pinghua, to not only inspire discussion, but to help all in China's education system to develop solutions.

Ray Hilsinger (Ai Xinren)

BA Cross-Cultural Communications
MA Cross-Cultural Communications

ACKNOWLEDGEMENTS

Sincere appreciation is extended to the following people who have helped in the development of this thesis.

I hereby extend my heartfelt gratitude to my supervisors, Dr Audrey Grant and Mr. Kevin Smith, for their invaluable advice, encouragement, and support in various ways, which have been indispensable to the completion of the dissertation.

I would like to thank Dr Lloyd Holliday and Professor Liu Shoulan for their constant encouragement, assistance, and helpful suggestions.

I must express my sincere appreciation to Ms. Erica Smith for her critical and valuable ideas on the structure and language of the dissertation.

I wish to thank Dr Janet Jamieson for reading this thesis for me and for her useful comments.

My appreciation is also extended to all those who helped me to find participants as well as the participants themselves.

Duan Pinghua

CONTENTS

SECTION A

TEFL and Beyond TEFL: Indicators of Creativity Among Chinese EFL Majors and Their Teachers

CHAPTER 1　INTRODUCTION ········· 3

  1.1　Introduction to the Study ········· 3
  1.2　Background of the Study ········· 4
  1.3　Overview of the Thesis ········· 6

CHAPTER 2　LITERATURE REVIEW ········· 8

  2.1　Introduction ········· 8
  2.2　Conceptual Disputes about Creativity ········· 8
  2.3　Creativity Hindering/ Fostering Factors ········· 14
  2.4　Content-Based Language Instruction ········· 19
  2.5　Summary and Research Questions ········· 22

CHAPTER 3　RESEARCH METHODOLOGY ········· 23

  3.1　Introduction ········· 23
  3.2　Rationale for Research Methodology ········· 23
  3.3　Working Model ········· 24
  3.4　Research Participants ········· 26
  3.5　Procedures ········· 29

3.6	Data Analysis	30
3.7	Limitation of the Research	32

CHAPTER 4　RESULTS AND DISCUSSIONS ... 33

4.1	Introduction	33
4.2	Key Informants' Stories and Emerging Themes	33
4.3	Factors Believed to Hinder/Foster Creativity	49
4.4	Indicators of Creativity Across Participants	54
4.5	Summary	59

CHAPTER 5　SUMMARY AND CONCLUSIONS ... 61

5.1	Introduction	61
5.2	Factors Seen to Hinder/Foster EFL Majors' Creativity	61
5.3	Indicators of Creative Potential and Creative Product	62
5.4	Pedagogical Implications	64
5.5	Proposal for Future Research	66

Appendix I	Questions for Semi-Structured Interview	75
Appendix II	Interview Transcript Sample	77

SECTION B

Theories and Practice:
Exploring Creative TEFL Methodology
in the Chinese Context

CHAPTER 1　CULTIVATING PLURALISTIC THINKING THROUGH LITERATURE TEACHING ... 87

1.1	Introduction	87
1.2	Students' Normal Response to "*Jane Eyre*"	88
1.3	Introducing Feminism Through "*Wide Sargasso Sea*"	89
1.4	Reviewing "*Jane Eyre*" from a Feminist's Point of View	91
1.5	Beyond Feminist Criticism	92

CHAPTER 2　MAXIMIZING THE EXPERTISE OF NATIVE ENGLISH SPEAKING TEACHERS IN CHINA　94

2.1　Introduction　94
2.2　The Study: Process and Results　95
2.3　Discussions　97
2.4　Minimize Disadvantages and Maximize Advantages　101

CHAPTER 3　RESPONDING TO FAVORS: A CONTRASTIVE STUDY OF GRATITUDE-EXPRESSING STRATEGIES BETWEEN CHINESE AND AMERICANS　106

3.1　Background　106
3.2　Methodology: Procedures and Limitations　109
3.3　Results of the Study and Preliminary Discussion　112
3.4　Cross-Cultural Discussion　116
3.5　Conclusion　119

Appendix I　Questionnaire for Americans　122

Appendix II　Answers Obtained from the Questionnaire for Americans　124

Appendix III　Questionnaire for Chinese Subjects　130

Appendix IV　English Translation Version of Questionnaire for Chinese Subjects　132

Appendix V　Answers Obtained from Questionnaire for Chinese Subjects　135

CHAPTER 4　TEXT PROCESSING AND LINGUISTIC BARRIERS FOR EFL LITERATURE READERS/LEARNERS　156

4.1　Introduction　156
4.2　Roles of Reader in Text Processing　157
4.3　Generation of Meaning from the Reader's World and Text World　159
4.4　Barriers for EFL Readers/learners in Text Processing　160
4.5　Brief Description of Research and Preliminary Discussion　162
4.6　More Findings　166
4.7　Vygotsky's Concept of Assistance in Dealing with the Linguistic Barriers and Propelling Intersection　168
4.8　Conclusion　170

CHAPTER 5 THE VALUE OF A "WEEKLY ENGLISH DAY" ········ 173
5.1　Introduction ··· 173
5.2　Why Do Traditional English Corners Fail? ················ 173
5.3　How Was the Weekly English Day Started? ··············· 174
5.4　Activities ·· 175
5.5　How Has the Weekly English Day Turned Out? ············ 177
5.6　Conclusion ·· 178

CHAPTER 6 A RESEARCH ON MONITORING SYSTEM OF ENLLIC ACQUISITION MODEL ································ 179
6.1　An Introduction to the Background ······················· 179
6.2　Research Methodology and Process ······················ 184
6.3　Data Collecting and Analyzing ··························· 190
6.4　Limitations of This Study and Suggestions for Further Research ········ 194
6.5　Conclusion ·· 195

SECTION A

TEFL and Beyond TEFL:
Indicators of Creativity
Among Chinese EFL
Majors and Their Teachers

英语教学课堂内外：
中国英语专业师生
创造性理念寻踪

CHAPTER 1　INTRODUCTION

1.1　Introduction to the Study

The current study has been carried out in response to a growing demand for change in education in China. In particular, it responds to an emerging recognition of the need to foster creativity amongst students majoring in English language and literature (henceforth English majors). The study attempts to identify indicators of creativity among English major students and teachers and to delineate positive and negative factors that are respectively seen to promote or constrain the expression of creativity in a Chinese EFL context. It further attempts to draw out some pedagogical implications that may provide teachers of English majors with a framework and strategies for fostering creativity amongst their students.

It must be stated from the outset that creativity is a contested notion, and that there does not appear to be any consensus on how to define creativity (Fleith, 2000). The review of literature (Chapter 2) notes definitions ranging from the categorization of creativity as personal traits and creative thinking process to the categorization of creativity as products. This study takes as its starting point Csikszentmihalyi's (1994) stance that creativity is a socially held concept and may vary in accordance with different domains and fields. This position is similar to the particular social and environmental factors which frame the Chinese EFL majors' expression of their creative potential in their specific cultural, educational and institutional context.

This study adopts a qualitative stance, drawing its insights from a series of semistructured interviews among Chinese informants (educational English majors and their teachers, tourism English majors and their teachers, and institutional administrators) from the same Foreign Languages Institution of a university in Yunnan, China. During these interviews, teachers and students were encouraged to tell their "stories of creativity" from their experiences of teaching and learning English. These "stories" elicited the interviewees' perceptions of creativity that were then analysed for indicators of creativity in a Chinese EFL context and, ultimately, form the basis for pedagogical implications.

1.2　Background of the Study

The Chinese determination to open China to the outside world in an attempt to catch up with the most advanced countries (Wan, 1999) has urged the Chinese nation to see a foreign language as "an essential tool in developing and changing the core of the country's economic system" (Burnaby & Sun, 1989: 221). Thus, the primary purpose of setting up foreign language major programs in Chinese universities and colleges is to accelerate China's communication with the outside world. Since the scope of services for foreign language professionals keeps widening, foreign language graduates should be able to stand at the forefront of China's reform and open policy. They should be able to play important roles in international communication and cooperation, in publicizing and obtaining information and scientific achievements, in developing administration and services, and in participating in education and scientific research work. As a result, the need for highly qualified foreign language speakers will continue to grow. This will be a challenge, as well as an opportunity for foreign language majors (Beifang Ketizhu, 1998).

As human society is undergoing massive change from its traditional industry based economy into an information-based economy in the 21st century, higher education in China clearly needs to cultivate high quality intellectuals who are not only knowledgeable in their own and related fields, but also creative and capable in problem-solving (Ren, 2001). Accordingly, qualified foreign language major graduates need to be open-minded, self-reliant, flexible and adaptable to social changes. They should have a solid foundation in education, a broad knowledge base and a mastery of their major foreign language (Nanfang Zhu, 1998).

English is the most widely learned foreign language in China. As Chinese people have long realized, among all the foreign languages, English is the "preferred language of world trade and commerce, science and technology and international relations" (Ford, 1988:4). It has become the dominant international language or "the international gatekeeper" (Pennycook, 1994: 18). The importance of the English language has been further accelerated up to and since China's entry into WTO, resulting in an increased demand for well qualified English professionals. Upon graduation, English majors should not only have competence in the language, but also a broad range of general knowledge, as well as advanced knowledge in a specific field. They should also possess the ability to acquire and use knowledge, problem identifying and solving ability, and creative ability (He, Yin, Huang, Liu, 1999).

However, current English major education in China, as a whole, seems to be "high in investment but low in production" (Zeng, 2000; Li & Liu, 2001). Liu (1999) observed that the practical or functional use of the language is usually neglected and the focus is often given to the form of the language in the actual practice of EFL. The result is poor use of the language. This situation is quite alarming. Many English major graduates seem unable to operate effectively in real communicative situations. Many often cannot translate properly a piece of text in practical situations. Zeng (2000) noted that it is no longer unusual to see that the English language competence of non-English major undergraduates far outreaches that of general English majors. On the other hand, many English majors may have good English competence, but are very narrow in their range of knowledge, poor in thinking and creative ability (Liu, 1999; Zeng, 2000).

The new national syllabus for English majors[1] (2000, hereafter referred to as "English Syllabus") requires that:

Some TEFL professionals (Zeng, 2000; He, Yin, Huang & Liu, 1999) are

---

[1] *Entrusted by Chinese National Education Committee, the first English Syllabus was edited by the English Group of the Tertiary Foreign Language Major Curriculum Editing Committee in the early 1980's and practiced throughout the country with the approval of the Tertiary Education Dept. of the National Education Committee. It had been regarded as the law to guide all the English Major education in China. Through the same official procedures and with the same function, the New English Syllabus was edited with a lot more careful work. The English Group consisted of 10 famous professors drafted the Syllabus first, and discussed it with representatives from more than 200 colleges and universities, then ratified it in its annual conference at the end of 1999. It was eventually approved by the Tertiary Education Dept. and put into practice in the year* 2000. The relationship between the training of the language competence and the cultivation of thinking and creative abilities should be properly handled in the teaching. Neither of them should be neglected (2000:12).

especially concerned about cultivating the thinking and creative abilities of students undertaking English major studies. Liu (2000) noted that the percentage of English major graduates who become outstanding in the academic world and practical work is quite low compared with graduates from other majors. He assumed that this phenomenon might be related to neglect in cultivating the students' creative and thinking ability and excessive concentration on the English language training.

Although few English majors would claim to be fully bilingual, research that focuses on creativity amongst bilinguals provides some worthwhile insights. Numerous international studies have shown positive results in bilinguals' creative ability. These indicate that bilingual children, relative to monolingual controls, show advantages on measures of cognitive flexibility, creativity, or divergent thinking (Balkan, 1970; Ianco-Worrall, 1972; Ben-Zeev, 1972, 1977; Cummins & Gulutsan, 1974; De Avila & Duncan, 1979). Second language learners were also found to score significantly higher than monolingual children in divergent thinking in figural tasks (Landry, 1973). The contradictory claim made by the Chinese educators regarding the English majors' creative ability is particularly baffling. Is it true? Why is it so? What kind of creative ability do they refer to? The concerns of the Chinese observers mentioned above need to be substantiated by further research. This study, therefore, attempts to provide some deeper insights into these issues. Specific focal questions of this study emerge from the review of literature and are proposed at the end of Chapter Two.

1.3 Overview of the Thesis

This opening chapter, Chapter One, identifies the research problem, introduces the situational contexts and outlines the major themes of the research.

Chapter Two provides a review of previous work relevant to the present study. It discusses different concepts about creativity and argues for the concept to be used as a framework in this research. Then the chapter reviews some current ideas about environmental factors that may hinder or foster the expression of students, especially that of Chinese students. Next, some pedagogical literature including content based English teaching methodology and its related EFL theories, which are related to creativity, are briefly discussed. The research questions derived from the literature review are presented at the end of this chapter.

Chapter Three discusses the methodological basis of the study. The chapter first argues for a particular methodology and explains how interviews based on qualitative theory were used to provide tentative answers relating to the major themes of the study. A working model for the current study is suggested and discussed. The chapter then describes how and why the informants were chosen, and provides a description of their general background. The chapter also explains the actual data collection and analysing procedures used and finish with an acknowledgement of the limitations of the study.

Chapter Four reports the findings from this study from three major perspectives: indicators of creativity which emerge from the English major students and teachers' interviews; factors that hinder/foster the English majors' creative potential in their education; and the pedagogical implications derived from the study.

Chapter Five concludes the thesis by outlining the major findings and implications of this study. Finally, suggestions for future research are offered.

CHAPTER 2 LITERATURE REVIEW

2.1 Introduction

The purpose of this chapter is to present a review of literature specifically related to the current thesis and to develop the research questions. Studies related to the conceptual disputes about creativity are reviewed. A theoretical framework for the initial conceptual study in this thesis is proposed in section 2.2. Then, creativity hindering and fostering factors are reviewed in section 2.3. In section 2.4, content based language instruction is examined. The chapter is summarized in section 2.5, and together with a reference to Chapter one, the research questions for this thesis are proposed.

2.2 Conceptual Disputes about Creativity

There does not seem to be consensus about how to define the term "creativity" (Fleith, 2000). The concept can be used either to "characterize a person" or to refer to the "successful outcome of some difficult endeavour that involves a measure of novelty" (Gedo, 2000:215). This section reviews various definitions of creativity from these two aspects. It first discusses the categorization of creativity as personal potential, and then creativity viewed as a product. After that, Csikszentmihalyi's (1994) notion of creativity as a set of social practices is discussed. At the end of this section, a working model for this study is formulated to gain insight into concepts of creativity held by English major teachers and students in a Chinese EFL (English as a Foreign Language) setting.

2.2.1 Creativity as personal potential

In this category of definitions, two sections are included: definitions focusing on creative personal traits and definitions concerning creative thinking processes. These two traditionally separate categories are placed together for two reasons. First, Guilford, the forefather of the field of creativity research in the modern era who has framed the majority of the studies on creativity (Guilford, 1950, cited in Feldman, Csikszentmihalyi, Gardner, 1994: 4 – 5), proposed studies in both categories. Secondly, both categories share one common feature that sets them apart from Csikszentmihalyi's model of creativity (see Section 2.2.3): they are only concerned with what happens in creative people's minds but in the absence of social and cultural stances. I give this category the name of "creativity as personal potential" as I believe that these personal traits or thinking features only provide the possibilities to create, but cannot ensure yielding creative products without taking into consideration supportive social and cultural environments and stances.

The definitions focusing on the creative person include three aspects: cognitive characteristics, personality including emotional qualities, and experiences in the midst of one's development (Tardiff & Sternberg, 1988). Such definitions specify that creativity is an individual ability or personal trait. Guilford (1950) first laid out the conceptual basis for creativity research in this direction by isolating factors of intellect and personality that creative individuals might possess.

In order to identify people's special personal properties believed to increase the likelihood of creativity, Kumar, Kemmler and Holman (1997) developed a Creativity Styles Questionnaire. The questionnaire measures seven dimensions: Belief in Unconscious Processes, Use of Techniques, Use of Other People, Final Product Orientation, Environmental Control, Superstition, and Use of Senses. Biographical inventories have been applied to find connections between creativity and personal experience, motivation. One of the best-known instruments of this kind is the Alpha Biographical Inventory designed by Taylor (Taylor & Ellison, 1968). It consists of 165 items focusing on factual information and measures five areas: family background (for example, educational level of parents), intellectual and social cultural orientation (for example, interests and hobbies, frequency of visits to museums or art galleries), motivation (for example, willingness to stay up very late on a work), breadth of interest (for example, number of hobbies pursued, number of favourite school subjects), and drive towards novelty and diversity (for example, level of interest in certain special art forms).

The category of definitions focusing on creative thinking processes is concerned with how to develop creative products that involve an original way to produce unusual ideas, to make different combinations, or to add new ideas to existing knowledge (Tardiff & Sternberg, 1988). Torrance (1962) defines creativity as the process of sensing gaps or missing elements and forming hypotheses concerning them, testing these hypotheses, communicating the results, and possibly modifying and retesting the hypotheses. Guilford (1967) defines creativity in terms of divergent thinking, which includes transformation, redefinition, and sensitivity to problems.

The most well known tests based on divergent thinking are the Torrance Tests of Creative Thinking that were first published in 1966 and revised afterwards (Torrance, 1999). Included in the test materials are a verbal section "Thinking Creatively with Words", and a nonverbal or figural section called "Thinking Creatively with Pictures". The verbal activities derive scores on three dimensions: Fluency, Flexibility, and Originality, while the nonverbal activities yield scores for five mental characteristics: Fluency, Originality, Elaboration, Abstractness of Titles, and Resistance to Premature Closure. Urban and Jellen's (1996) *Test of Creative Thinking* (Divergent Production) yields scores from "image production". Respondents' productions are rated according to dimensions of Boundary Breaking, New Elements, and Humour and Affectivity. Respondents are offered a sheet of paper containing incomplete figures and make drawing(s) containing the fragments, in whatever way they wish. *The Creative Reasoning Test* was designed by Doolittle (1990) to test participants' problem-solving ability. The problems to be solved are presented in the form of riddles, and participants are supposed to find the correct answers for them. The participants' answers are then scored according to a standard scoring key.

To sum up, the definitions of creativity that focus on personal creative potential (whether personal traits or thinking process) and the studies tied to these definitions have provided a valuable means of viewing creativity. However, since they are only concerned with what happens in creative people's minds, in the absence of supportive social and cultural environments and stances, they are less likely to properly explain the occurrence of creative products.

2.2.2 Creativity as product

The definitions that focus on the characteristics of the creative product make the point that the product must be new and useful. Creative Product Semantic Scale, as developed by Besemer and O'Quin (1987), caters for the study of creative product on three dimensions: Novelty (the product is original, surprising and germinal), Resolution (the product is valuable, logical, useful, and understandable), and Elaboration and Synthesis (the product is organic, elegant, complex, and well-crafted).

According to the level of the creative product, creativity can be either "small" or "big". Big creativity is "the achievement of something remarkable and new, something which transforms and changes a field of endeavour in a significant way", while small creativity can be "a charming arrangement of fresh flowers to brighten up a room, or the use of a doorstop to weatherstrip an ill-fitting window, or a clever remark that lightens the tone of a conversation" (Feldman, Csikszentmihalyi & Gardner, 1994:2).

The use of creative product as a means of measurement indicates the belief that people's creative potential can be assessed through the type of product they yield. Mayer (1999) observes that although there has been no consensus as to whether creativity is located in a person, a process, or a product, it is generally accepted that novelty and value should be the basic criteria for a creative product. Also, it is usually through the creative product that a creative person is identified and studied. Thus, the product may not only indicate the characteristics of the creative product itself, but signpost personal creative potential as well. That is why, in this study, I frequently attempt to draw on Chinese EFL major participants' reports regarding the ideas, events or activities that they believe to be creative. In this way, more panoramic views of their understandings about creativity are elicited: both understandings in creative potential and creative product, and whether "big" or "small" creativity.

However, what are the criteria adopted to evaluate creative product? Who sets these evaluating criteria? Csikszentmihalyi and Robinson (1988) maintain that the study of creativity should not disregard social judgment. They propose a wellknown DIFI (Domain Individual Field Interaction) framework, as will be discussed in the section which follows.

2.2.3 Creativity as a set of social practices

Csikszentmihalyi (1994), who spent twenty-five years studying creative people's personality traits and cognitive processes, makes the following remarks:

> The more I tried to say the "creative people are such and such" or "creative people do this and that," the less sure I became about what creativity itself consisted of and how we could even begin to figure out what it was.(Csikszentmihalyi, 1994:135)

Later on, Csikszentmihalyi concludes, "Creativity is not an attribute of individuals but of social systems making judgments about individuals" (Csikszentmihalyi, 1994:144). He proposes a dynamic DIFI framework that consists of three primary subsystems that interact with each other: individual, domain, and field. By "domain", he means the "formally organized body of knowledge that is associated with a given field." "Field" is defined as "all those persons who can affect the structure of a domain." The person has traditionally been the focus of creativity research. However, to study individual creativity without considering domain and field is just like "trying to understand how an apple tree produces fruit by looking only at the tree and ignoring the sun and the soil that support its life (Csikszentmihalyi, 1994:146)." The DIFI framework (Figure 2-1) suggests that

> ...individuals acquire knowledge of challenging domains, eventually propose new knowledge for those domains, and have the potential new knowledge considered by the field. If the proposed new knowledge is accepted by the field, it becomes part of it and is added to the domain, it will contain the new element contributed by individuals who have acquired the knowledge of the domain at an earlier point (Feldman, Csikszentmihalyi & Gardner, 1994:20).

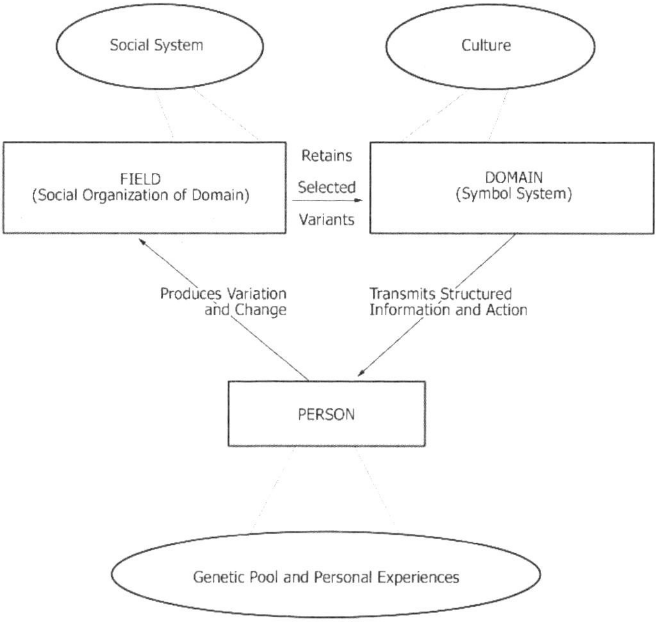

```
                  Social System                    Culture

                              Retains
          FIELD              Selected         DOMAIN
(Social Organization of Domain)               (Symbol System)
                              Variants

        Produces Variation          Transmits Structured
          and Change                Information and Action

                         PERSON

             Genetic Pool and Personal Experiences
```

Figure 2-1   The locus of creativity
(Copied from M. Csikszentmihalyi 1988:329)

This model has taken into account only "big" creativity (Section 2.2.2), and thus does not quite fit into the current study. However, it provides an essential notion for this research, namely, that the social criteria of a particular field should be considered and the knowledge of the domain is needed for creativity to take place. According to this model, the English language and literature field in China, just like any other field, may have its own criteria for judging creativity: personal creative potential or creative product. What are these standards in the English language and literature field in China? Is the creative ability as suggested by English Syllabus designers the same as that understood by the English majors and teachers, who constitute the actual syllabus performers? This thesis seeks to gain insights relating to the concept of creativity held by the English major undergraduates and teachers. Although this study adopts Csikszentmihalyi's basic notion that creativity is a socially and culturally held concept depending on the judgments of a specific field, it is not to be limited in the sole pursuit for "big" creativity. The study will take into account creativity as product: whether "big" or "small" (Section 2.2.2), and creativity as personal potential: whether personal traits or thinking process. These speculations are summarized in an initial working model of creativity generated for this study (Refer to Figure 2-2).

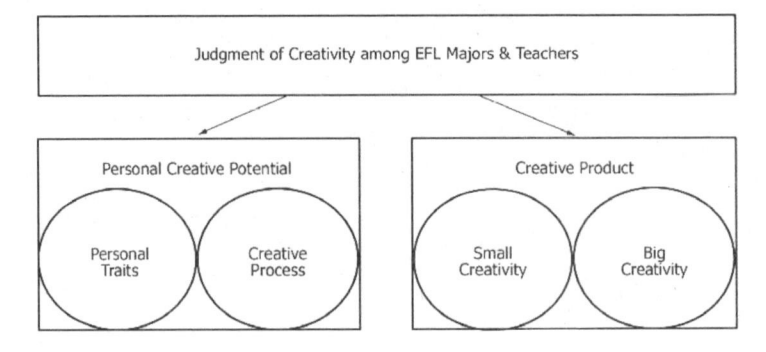

Figure 2-2　Concept of creativity held by English majors and their teachers

2.3　Creativity Hindering/ Fostering Factors

This section first reviews some findings that are believed to be either creativity fostering or hindering in the school environment. Then examples of hindrances found to be existent in the traditional Chinese culture and the Chinese school environment in particular are discussed.

2.3.1　Factors that hinder/foster creativity in school settings

Some studies have explored the relationship between school environment and students' creativity. Clearly, this is significant in the specific Chinese institutional context of the present study. Dudek, Strobel and Runco (1993) examined the influence of school environment on the creative potential of fifth and sixth grade students from eleven schools in Montreal. The results showed that the global climate of a school, such as the socio-economic level and classroom differences within the same socio-economic level schools, significantly influenced students' creative performance. They also found that the social dynamics prevailing in a classroom, comprising student-teacher composition and interactions between them, also seemed to have an impact on students' expression of creativity.

Sternberg and Williams (1996) proposed that in the educational setting, an environment that fosters creativity should include the following components: giving time to do creative thinking; rewarding creative performances; pushing reasonable risks; permit-ting mistakes; imagining other opinions; exploring the surroundings; showing doubts in assumptions.

Soh (2000) particularly emphasized the significant role a teacher plays in fostering student creativity:

> A teacher can directly reinforce creativity through her interaction with students by rewarding their creative efforts (process) and outcomes (product) as well as recognizing their creative traits (person). The teacher can also indirectly influence student creativity by creating a supportive social environment through her words and deeds (Soh, 2000: 119).

Therefore, the teacher's responses in relation to student creativity may enable students to be motivated to create and be creative. Thus they will be conscious of how their teacher reacts to their performances as a signal concerning the acceptability of their creative efforts and output (Soh, 2000).

After discussion on the various conditions and factors of student creativity, Cropley (1997, cited in Soh, 2000: 119 – 120) listed the following teacher's classroom behavior as creativity fostering:

1. Encouraging (sic) students to learn independently.
2. Have a co-operative, socially integrative style of teaching.
3. Motivate their students to master factual knowledge, so that they have a solid base for divergent thinking.
4. Delay judging students' ideas until they have been thoroughly worked out and clearly formulated.
5. Encourage flexible thinking.
6. Promote self-evaluation in students.
7. Take students' suggestions and questions seriously.
8. Offer students opportunities to work with a wide variety of materials and under many different conditions.
9. Help students to learn to cope with frustration and failure, so that they have the courage to try the new and unusual (Cropley, 1997, cited in Soh, 2000:119-120).

Factors that hinder creativity in the educational settings were also noted and studied by some researchers. According to Amabile (1989, cited in Fleith, 2000:

2), "evaluation, competition, restricted choices, conformity pressure, frequent failures and rote learning" can destroy creativity in school. Kramer-Dahl (1997, cited in Koh, 2002:260) also discovered that the "entrenched mindset of teachers indoctrinated by an examination-oriented syllabus could strongly resist adopting critical English teaching pedagogy". Torrance (1983) points out that an overemphasis upon memorization has resulted in negligence in cultivating children's creative thinking. All these creativity-hindering factors sound very familiar in the Chinese educational system. The next section focuses on Chinese cultural and educational traditions that hinder creativity.

2.3.2 Chinese cultural and educational traditions that hinder creativity

According to Maslow (1970), creativity is a potentiality present in all people at birth, but most human beings lose it as they became "encultured". Section 2.3.2.1

discusses some Chinese cultural and educational traditions that hinder the expression of creativity. General Chinese cultural factors that hinder creativity are discussed first. Then, Chinese traditional teaching and learning styles are discussed in particular in Section 2.3.2.2, followed by a discussion about backwash effects of the tests taking place in Chinese education in 2.3.2.3.

2.3.2.1 Hierarchy and extreme conformity: Chinese cultural blocks to creativity

The feudal Chinese society was basically a hierarchical society like a huge clan, in which all those above you, including your elders, teachers and higher-ranking officials, were looked on as "superiors". You could not disagree with them in any respect, or you would be regarded as immoral. This relational and ethical system is still highly valued in Chinese society today, where much belief is given to authority and seniority, and little to real ability and selfhood. As a result, the individual easily becomes an obedient follower with no value system of his or her own and no independent thinking. He/she loses him/herself in the submission to authority and seniority and thus loses his/her creativity (Wang, 1988). On the contrary, creative people are likely to be independent thinkers who are on the nonconformist side with their own criteria of value (Guilford, 1967:318).

Extreme conformity was used as an effective tool to help the emperors to keep control of the big population in the old China. With the collapse of feudalist society, however, the influence of extreme conformity has not disappeared (Wang, 1988:

11). There are five major channels through which extreme conformity functions on individuals in Chinese society: "model-establishing", "mass media", "education system", "colleagues (or peers)" and "the penalty of non-conformism" (Wang, 1988:10-27). Among all of the cultural blocks to creativity, he believes that the high pressure towards extreme conformity is the most important one. With the great pressure towards extreme conformity, the Chinese individual has to make use of ego defense mechanisms, an individual's strategy to "defend against open expressions of id impulses and opposing superego pressures" (Hjelle & Ziegler, 1976:127). Conse-quently, his or her ego, "the seat of intellect", would be greatly repressed by his or her superego that "represents an internalised version of society's norms and standards of behaviour" (Hjelle & Ziegler, 1976:127). In the words of Anderson's (1959:138), "all uses of force, coercion, domination, shame, blame, guilt" result from extreme conformity and would cause the "the stifling of the creative process, the annihilation of originality."

2.3.2.2 Chinese teaching and learning tradition

In China, teachers are traditionally considered as a model, a knowledge transmitter, a learning guide, an authority, an expert, and a nurturer (Byron & Macmillan; 1990, Paine; 1990, Ross, 1993), and students as a receiver, a follower, an apprentice, and an audience (Paine, 1990; Brick, 1991; Gao, 1993). With this learning blueprint in mind, teachers are socially expected to be responsible for students' progress and achievements (Brick, 1991, Ross, 1993), and decide what to teach and how to teach through the use of textbooks (Ting, 1987). This firmly rooted, unquestionable role of Chinese teachers in relation to their students (Orton, 1990; Flowerdew & Miller, 1995) has fostered and maintained the adoption of a teacher-centred lecture style so that teachers feel they have taught their students knowledge (Orton, 1990), and "declining a request to lecture is often interpreted by the students as a demonstration of a lack of knowledge" (Yu, 1984:36) As a result of such a practice, Chinese students, who traditionally see themselves as part of the hierarchy, also rarely find autonomy comfortable (Ho & Crookall, 1995), and the teachers' authority and the students' over-reliance on the teacher have been constantly reinforced.

Knowledge is believed to reside in the teacher-expert (Craig, 1995) and in the text, "the core" in teaching and learning (Zhang et al., 1993:196). Textbooks, as well as teachers, are viewed as the main sources of knowledge (Harvey, 1985; Paine, 1992). Since textbooks are considered as a central part of the students' learning, teachers' authority is established and based on their profound knowledge of the prescribed texts and their techniques in disseminating it (Sun & Wu, 1986) through the use of "cramming" teaching methodology (Chen, 1998).

The reverence with which many Chinese treat books has pushed the students to learn by heart what they contain (Maley, 1986: 103). Recitation, memorization, imitation, repetition and analogising are believed to be key approaches to language learning in China (Hu, 1994; Cortazzi & Jin, 1996). In comparing the Chinese and Western culture of learning a foreign language, Cortazzi and Jin (1996: 199) noted that Chinese culture "emphasizes knowledge of vocabulary and grammar, and the result of learning", while Westerners "stress communicative skills, language use and the process of learning".

2.3.2.3 Tests and test backwash

China maintains a highly centralised educational system that was primarily constructed on the Soviet model in which state control and authority have played a crucial role (Bastid, 1987; Porter, 1990; Szalay et al., 1994; Li & Walkers, 1997). China's primary and secondary education has now fallen into a crazy competition for the National College Entrance Examination.[①] The unified National College Entrance Exams and the unified textbooks have given no room for schools and teachers to organize their own teaching. School hours for students have been greatly increased to an almost inhuman extent. Thus,

> Most students have to give up or maybe have never had any of their personal interests out of study. They have no time to digest what they have been taught, no time to imagine and no time to think for themselves. They work with full attention for so long that their unconscious, the major source of creativity, will never have a chance to come up to help. And also as all of their learning activities and, of course, all of the teaching activities are programmed for the national competition, which only tests convergent

---

① *In China, all students who wish to study at colleges or universities, especially prestigious ones, have to pass a series of nation-wide tests designed according to the academic standards required by the nationally unified syllabus and textbooks. Since there are always more students who wish to attend colleges than the actual positions available, a heated competition is formed that involve all the parties related to tests.*

thinking, then their divergent thinking ability has been greatly reduced nearly to zero. (Wang, 1988:47-48)

As a result of this national competition, a serious of problems in education of "High marks but low ability" has emerged as a major concern for the government and educators. Many students can achieve high marks in exams but have very low ability in practice. They are short of the courage, the impulse and the method for creativity.

Other than the macro-social and actual school environment, some Chinese observers (as discussed in Section 1.2) indicate that the process of learning English could affect the expression of the English majors' creativity (Liu, 1999; Zeng, 2000). It is the main interest of this study to further explore the actual creativity hindering and fostering situations in which the education of the Chinese English major take place.

To sum up, this section has reviewed some opinions and some studies that have been accomplished regarding the environmental factors, especially those in school, in relation to one's expression of creative potential. The literature shows that creation of an enhancing, harmonious and meaningful environment can contribute to the expression of students' creative potential, while some traditional Chinese cultural factors, especially those in school settings, can hinder students' creativity. However, so far, much more research effort has been directed to product, person, and process but much less to environmental pressure (Soh, 2000). This thesis hopes to gain some useful insights from the English major students and teachers into what they believe to be factors that foster/hinder creativity in their EFL settings.

2.4 Content-Based Language Instruction

Liu (1999) thinks that for EFL beginners, teaching materials may have to include 100% of language elements and 0% of content, but the percentage of content in TEFL has to be increased with the improvement of their language competence. Advanced EFL learners may have to involve 80% of meaningful information and only 20% of the language emphasis. Shih (1999:20) also suggests that when students reach college or university level, "their focus should shift from learning about the English language to using English to learn and communicate about topics that are interesting and relevant to their lives". In TEFL, the teachers need to attract their students with the power of knowledge and content, and "conquer" them with wisdom (Liu, 1999).

Regarding the traditional means of removing students from the mainstream and giving them intensive courses to develop their English language skills, Tang (1997: 69) considers that this practice is "marginalized" and "segregated". He is concerned that it "denies students the full benefits of education, that is, full access to content area subject matter and, possibly, development of thinking skills."

Widdowson (1968, 1978) was one of the first to suggest that language teaching might be totally integrated with content teaching, and that English could be acquired through the medium of some other subjects. About the relationship between language and content, he (Widdowson 1990:103) maintains that:

> The effectiveness of language teaching will depend on what is being taught, other than language, that will be recognized by the learners as a purposeful and relevant extension of their schematic horizons.

Mohan (1986) has stressed the potential of integrating language and content, pointing out that such a procedure has the advantage of not only helping students to learn a language, but also teaching them how to use the language to learn.

Spanos (1987:229) presents a list of conditions that content-based language teaching should fulfil on the basis of Brinton, Snow, and Wesche (1989):

* Language teaching should be related to the eventual uses to which the learner will put the language.
* The use of informational content tends to increase the motivation of the language learner.
* Effective teaching requires attention to prior knowledge, existing knowledge, the total academic environment, and the linguistic proficiency of the learner.
* Language teaching should focus on contextualized language use rather than on sentence level usage.
* Language learning is promoted by a focus on significant and relevant content from which learners can derive the cognitive structures that facilitate the acquisition of vocabulary and syntax as well as written and oral production.

(Spanos, 1987:229)

The role of content, however, has been the subject of debate, for instance, what kind of content and how much of it belongs in language classes, how language teachers might learn it (Braine, 1988; Liebman-Kleine, 1986; Reid, 1984). In response to debates over content, Pally (1997) had recommended sustained content study, which was later phrased sustained content language teaching (SCLT) by Murphy and Stoller (2001:3-5). SCLT has two major components:

1. a focus on the exploration of a single content area, or carrier topic
2. a complementary focus on L2 learning and teaching

(Murphy & Stoller, 2001:3)

The challenge that SCLT teachers face is to coordinate both content and language teaching efficiently with the search to balance these two components being the key issue of SCLT (Murphy & Stoller, 2001:4).

As discussed in 2.2, knowledge of a domain is the source for creativity. Thus, content-based language instruction sounds quite promising in TEFL, as it provides the learners a content which they can use to build their creativity. Content-based language instruction is supported by Krashen's (1982, 1983, 1985) argument that language can only be best acquired in natural settings when provided with "comprehensible input". While the teacher makes comprehensible to the learner the meanings in the content text, and the learner is engaged in grasping the content, a close to real language acquisition environment is formed with information that is comprehensible to the learner.

To sum up, if properly applied, content-based language instruction may not only help EFL students to learn English well, it would also assist the students to build up their content knowledge as a basis for creativity. This study, therefore, seeks greater understanding of pedagogical issues relating to how the Chinese EFL major students respond to their teachers of English who are more inclined to content-based language instruction.

2.5 Summary and Research Questions

This chapter has reviewed different ways of defining creativity. Csikszentmihalyi's notion of creativity as a result of dynamic social judgment emerges as a most appropriate starting point. Based on this, an initial working model has been formed for the current research. The working model shows that this study hopes to explore the understanding of Chinese EFL majors and their teachers' about creativity, including personal creative potential (whether personal traits or thinking process) and creative product (whether "big" or "small"). The second section of this chapter has also reviewed some findings that are believed to foster or hinder students' creativity in the school environment. Then some hindrances to creativity, which are deeply embedded in the traditional Chinese culture and the Chinese school environment in particular, have been discussed. The third section has reviewed content-based language instruction. This section of the review is deemed to be important because inclusion of TEFL courses that emphasize content area learning may provide a possible means to build students' content knowledge for creativity without having to take away from the time devoted to improving their English competence.

The current study chooses to start by locating the indicators of creativity among the participants of the English major program, intending to find from their elicited stories factors that hinder/foster the students' creativity, with the hope of gaining some practical insights to modify the program.

Three major research questions are posed:

1. What are indicators of creativity (creative product and creative potential) according to the English language and literature major undergraduates and teachers?

2. According to EFL major participants, what are the factors that hinder or foster TEFL majors' creativity present in the current English major program?

3. What implications can be drawn for Chinese EFL major education to foster the students' creativity in their TEFL courses?

To explore these issues, an appropriate research methodology is needed. The following chapter provides a description of and the rationale for the research methods used in this research.

CHAPTER 3 RESEARCH METHODOLOGY

3.1 Introduction

This chapter explains the rationale for qualitative research methodology and, in particular, the use of semi-structured interviews for this study. Then I present a working model to signal how the research was carried out in order to achieve the purpose of the study. Next, I describe the research participants and elucidate the procedures and data analysis process. Finally, the limitations of the present study are outlined.

Since the focus in the chapter is on what I as researcher do, I have chosen to write in the first person.

3.2 Rationale for Research Methodology

Qualitative research is a situated activity that locates the observer in the world. It consists of a set of interpretive, material practices that make the world visible. These practices transform the world. They turn the world into a series of representations including field notes, interviews, conversations, photographs, recording, and memos to the self (Denzin & Lincoln, 2000:3).

Qualitative research methodology was the key feature of this study. The nature of research design and method should be determined by the objectives of the research and the research problems (Burns, 1994). Larsen-Freeman and Long (1991:14) also makes the point that "the methodological design should be determined by the research question". As indicated in the research questions, I am mainly concerned with the participants' notions of creativity and insights in fostering English majors' creative potential. This conceptual and pedagogical research necessarily involves complicated issues. A qualitative mode enabled me, as the researcher, to focus on and to explore the complexities of the research problems rooted in the social fabric (Burns, 1994; Lazaraton, 1995).

Interviews enable the researcher to have access to an interviewee's values, understandings, beliefs and attitudes (Tuckman, 1972). Instead of being a neutral tool of data gathering, interviews are being increasingly used to enable active interactions between two (or more) people leading to negotiated, contextually based results (Fontana & Frey, 2000).

Since the semi-structured interview is often designed without fixed wording and ordering of questions, it provides a much more flexible version of the structured interview. The semi-structured interview "permits greater flexibility than the closeended type and permits a more valid response from the informant's perception of reality" (Burns, 1994). It helps the researcher to achieve a greater depth of study by probing into the issues being discussed and negotiated (Hitchcock & Hughes, 1989). The semi-structured interview is of an open-ended nature in which the researcher can ask the respondents' views, opinions, suggestions, and get insights into certain issues (Yin, 1989). The respondent is free to talk about what is of central significance to him/her, and to move freely from one topic to another, within the guided framework (Bell, 1987). The way in which semi-structured interviews were implemented in this study is explained in detail in Section 3.5.

3.3 Working Model

Scholars in the social sciences tend to apply research approaches which lead to develop interpretative understanding of human beings, since "human beings are viewed as interpretative beings, inescapably involved in making sense of their experience, in connecting human actions to their meanings, to what they signify"

(Grant, 1997:35). Grant (1997:36) cites White's (1995) notion of "story or narrative as life" as follows,

> This is to propose that human beings are interpreting beings—that we are active in the interpretation of our experiences as we live our lives. It is to propose that it's not possible for us to interpret our experience without access to some frame of intelligibility, one that makes the attribution of meaning possible. It is to propose that stories constitute this frame of intelligibility (White, 1995, cited in Grant, 1997:36)

Rosen (1993:149) also states that "storytelling is an essential part of the functioning of the human mind. It is a major means of thinking and communicating our thoughts".

Throughout the research, it was my primary interest to explore the participants' (whether teachers or students) notions about creativity and pedagogical insights. In order to obtain these goals, I did not ask them direct questions. Instead, I enabled them to recount narratives about their teachers or students, friends, and about themselves; stories about their hopes and despair, their likes and dislikes, anything that might result in references to creativity.

As the participants often became more emotional and more talkative about some questions that directly involve themselves, rich and interesting data also emerged pertaining to other themes that I had not intended. For example, when I asked Xiao Yang (EES2) to tell me her own stories of being creative, my primary intention was to extract tacit concepts about creativity. However, as she told me her own experience of being creative, she also recounted the background relating to the creative ideas that occurred to her, then continued talking about particular courses or teachers she liked. Interwoven in her stories were also instances when her classmates had been observed to be creative. With such data, I would be allowed to locate not only Xiao Yang's indicators about creative product and personal potential, but socio-cultural insights and pedagogical implications as well. Therefore, the interview questions with implicit purposes proved to have multiple outcomes in actual practice. They functioned effectively to elicit a range of rich data. A basic model, which attempts to encompass the overall of factors elicited in this study, has been shaped and formulated in Figure 3-1.

Basically, by eliciting the participants' stories about creative persons or products, I was aiming for two layers of data. On the upper layer of the data were situations where creativity took place or did not occur. These data provided immediate factors seen to have fostered or hindered the TEFL major undergraduates' creativity. On the lower layer of the data, from the ways that they told these stories, indicators of creative product and personal creative potential were available to give insights about their understanding in creativity. The informants' stories about creative personal traits and creative products could also suggest pedagogical practices.

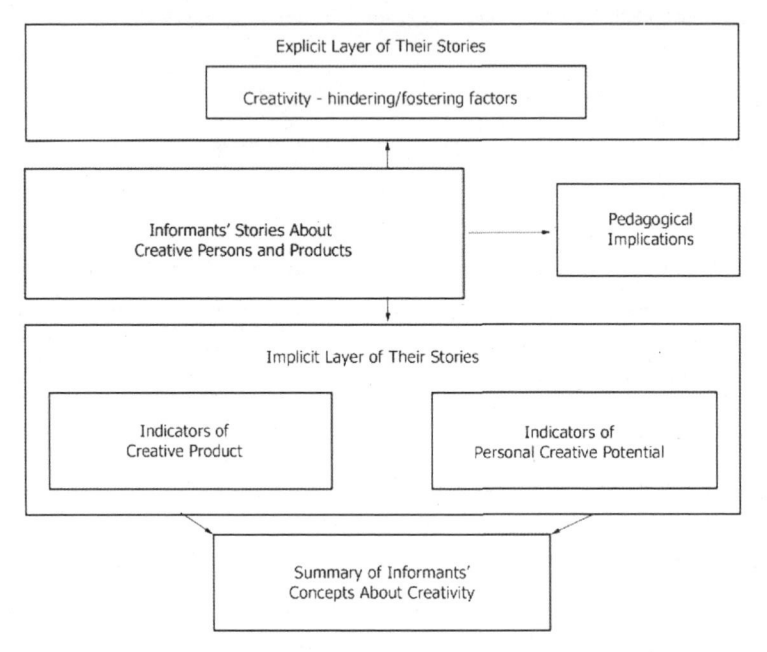

Figure 3-1 Working model for interviews in this study

3.4 Research Participants

In line with the research purposes, representing five groups altogether 18 research participants, were involved in the semi-structured interview: 7 educational English major students, 4 tourism English major students, 2 educational English major teachers, 3 tourism English teachers, and 2 institutional administrators. Table 3-1 presents a summary of background information on these participants, all of whom are from the same school of foreign languages in a university in Yunnan, China.

Both tourism English majors and educational English majors are grouped together for the purpose of the research, as many of their course units are taken in common. The major purpose of their study in both groups is to ensure that they gain good English language competence. Their EFL textbooks and class time do not have major differences. These EFL courses include Comprehensive English, Extensive English, English Listening, Oral English, Translation, and English Grammar. However, as their names suggest, tourism English majors are supposed to be involved in the tourism industry while educational English majors are expected to become English teachers after their graduation, and in order to prepare the undergraduates for their respective future careers, apart from the EFL courses and several other commonly shared courses, the institute also offers them specific courses relating to their vocational needs. The educational English majors are required to take a course called "TEFL Methodologies", while the tourism English majors are required to learn "English Tour Guide Operations", "Hotel Operation and Management", "Travel Service Operation", "Tour Guide Speeches", "Yunnan Provincial Information". In addition, the tourism English majors are required to pass a series of provincial-level tests to obtain two licenses before their graduation: Chinese Mandarin Tour Guide License and English Tour Guide License.

I chose year-3 undergraduates (at the end of their year-3 and beginning of their year-4 study) as my student informants because they had already completed more than half of their college studies as English majors and therefore represented a relatively stable group from which to elicit interview data.

Apart from the institutional administrators, all the other participants were chosen by nomination. Two students, who were considered by their teachers to be more "talkative", were chosen as beginning participants. But in order to avoid the teachers' biases, the following students were each nominated by the preceding ones. The request was put at the end of the interview with him or her: "Who would you recommend I interview next so that I can find out more, or different ideas?" The procedure is similar to that outlined by Guba&Lincoln (1989) whereby a hermeneutic circle of research is established. This is process whose main purpose is "not to justify one's own construction or attack other construction but to form a connection among them that allows their mutual exploration by all parties" (Guba & Lincoln, 1989:149). The teachers most frequently mentioned by the students during interviews were chosen as my teacher informants. I stopped interviewing more participants when I found that no further new ideas were emerging, and "recurrent affirmations" (Leininger, 1994) of previous material indicated that a level of "saturation" had been reached. There were not many institutional administrators to choose from. In fact, the division between teachers and administrators is not obvious. Both of the administrator participants also teach students some Chinese courses but they have to dedicate most of their working hours to administration in their respective offices. Meanwhile, one of the teacher interviewees also holds an important administrative responsibility; just that she does not have to stay in the office after her class time, like most other full-time teachers. For the purpose of this study, I do not feel it necessary to separate the administrators from the teacher participants in the discussions.

The table below summarizes background information on participants in the study:

Table 3-1 Backgrounds of Participants

Participant Stratifications		Sex M	Sex F	BA Candidate	BA	MA Candidate	MA	Age 20-35	Age 35-50	Age 50-65	Admin. Position	Code
Tourism English Major Sector (Year-3)	Teachers		√				√		√		√	TET1
			√			√		√				TET2
			√			√		√				TET3
	Students		√	√				√				TES1
			√	√				√				TES2
			√	√				√				TES3
			√	√				√				TES4
English Education Major Sector (Year-3)	Teachers		√				√		√			EET1
		√			√				√			EET2
	Students		√	√				√			√	EES1
			√	√				√				EES2
		√		√				√			√	EES3
		√		√				√			√	EES4
			√	√				√				EES5
			√	√				√				EES6
		√		√				√				EES7
Institutional Administrators			√		√			√		√		TA1
		√			√				√	√		TA2
Total		5	13	11	3	2	2	13	4	1	6	18

3.5 Procedures

Semi-structured interviews were carried out individually for more than half an hour on the average with each of the 18 participants. In order to ensure maximum opportunity for expression of the interviewees' ideas or experiences, I carried out all of the interviews in Chinese, our shared mother tongue.

Fontana and Frey (2000) warned, "Asking questions and getting answers is a much harder task than it may seem at first". The quality of the information obtained from the interview is largely dependent on how the interviewer handles it. He or she needs to make it possible for the person being interviewed to bring him or her into the "interviewee's world" (Patton, 1990:279). In order to ensure success, questions and settings for interviews were carefully planned. Considerable attention was paid to the establishment of affinity, empathy, and understanding between the interviewees and me as the interviewer (Hitchcock & Hughes, 1989). Non-threatening, encouraging, polite and genial interaction and interpersonal skills are the key to a successful survey (Lofland, 1971). Therefore, the interviewer ought to be courteous, friendly, and pleasant:

> He [sic] should be neither too grim nor too effusive; neither too talkative nor too timid. The idea should be to put the respondent at ease, so that he [sic] will talk freely and fully.
> (Selltiz, Jahoda, Deutsch & Cook, 1965:576)

Considering the traditional Chinese hierarchical teacher-student relationship that might hinder the student participants' free and full expression, in my interviews with them, I tried several things to ensure a relaxed atmosphere. First of all, before formal interviews, I carried on small talk with them. I did not start asking the intended questions until I felt that my informants were fully relaxed. Also, I introduced myself to the student interviewees as an MA candidate rather than as a teacher with more than 16 years experience. I also assured them that I would keep their identities anonymous and that they could say whatever they had in mind.

Since interviews involve the researcher's direct contacts with the informants, it is of vital importance that the researcher be fully aware of the impact of the researcher's subjective world, so as to deliberately avoid researcher biases (Bogdan & Biklen, 1982; Bell, 1987; Diesing, 1971, Tuckman, 1972). In the whole process of the interviews, I was particularly prudent not to let my own biases, opinions and emotions affect my behaviour. In order to achieve this, not only did I try to phrase my questions in the least biased ways, but I also tried to avoid expressing my opinions before I was sure that the interviewees had quite fully expressed themselves. Throughout the interviews, I played the role of a good listener and always showed great interest in what the interviewees said by using encouraging body language and appreciative short comments. I rarely interrupted when they were eager to talk about something. I only intervened when they obviously drifted too far away. My belief is that no data should be regarded as insignificant until they are transcribed and interpreted. As a result, I learned greatly by listening to the flow of their stories, and it also allowed me to explore more thoroughly the interviewees' implicit ideas and feelings in the actual data analysis.

Overall I felt I was very effective in eliciting my informants' ideas in some depth. Some even apologized afterwards that they had talked too much and several indicated that they would enjoy having another talk with me later. Obviously, that was what I, as the interviewer had hoped for.

3.6 Data Analysis

In qualitative interviews, data analysis should be done simultaneously with data collection so that the researcher can focus and shape the study as it proceeds. The data should be consistently organized and reflected upon to discover the meaning (Glesne & Peshkin, 1992). A large quantity of tape recordings of interviews was transcribed and carefully examined in different stages and changes were made to the questions to further fine tune later interviews as they went along. Glaser (1978, cited in Bogdan & Biklen, 1992: 74) recounts the process of data collection, data analysis, and continuous shaping of categories as follows:

1. Begin collecting data.

2. Look for key issues, recurrent events, or activities in the data that become categories of focus.

3. Collect data that provide many incidents of the categories of focus with an eye to seeing the diversity of the dimensions under the categories.

4. Write about the categories you are exploring, attempting to describe and account for all the incidents you have in your data while continually searching for new incidents.

5. Work with the data and emerging model to discover basic social processes and relationships.

6. Engage in sampling, coding, and writing as the analysis focuses on the core categories.

(cited in Bogdan & Biklen, 1992:74).

Reading and rereading the transcripts alone was not enough, though. I found that listening to the original recording over and over again was also quite necessary to gain holistic understanding about the interviews. Hesitations, changes in the mood, speed and tones of the speech may not be fully interpreted and transcribed. Listening to the tapes in combination with reading the transcripts greatly helped me to recall the holistic situation at the interviewing site and, in many cases, assisted me to gain more understanding beneath the interviewees' superficial wording. When I lacked confidence about some analysis that I had done on my own, I also called the particular interviewees to ask for their clarification. Only by doing so was I able to adequately identify the emerging themes and the general units of meaning for further evidence and clarification.

Of the 18 interviewees, the interview data of two key informants were chosen to enable me to develop a framework of "indicators of creativity". This process was deemed to be fundamentally important because I needed a basis for analysing the large amount of data collected. One teacher informant (EET1) and one student informant (EES3) were selected for this procedure as the interview data from these two were deemed to be very comprehensive. The actual search for and identification of the indicators was carried out inductively and is described hereunder. Once a basic framework of indicators was identified through this inductive process from the data of the two key informants, the resulting framework was then used to analyze the interview data from all interviewees.

This identifying process is very time-consuming and necessitates great patience as well as full concentration. I also realized the importance of keeping the source indicators and the ones identified in different interviews consistent throughout the data analysis stage in Chinese—the language in which all the interviews had been carried out. It was only after all the procedures were finished did I begin to sort out a proper translation of the indicators in English.

3.7 Limitation of the Research

The limitations of this study are acknowledged below.

First of all, since the distinctive contribution of qualitative research as a whole and of semi-structured interviews in particular exists in the analysis of complicated situations, involvement of various topics related to the conceptual discussion is unavoidable. As a qualitative researcher and a TEFL teacher, I found it hard to disregard "gold nuggets" on the way, either conceptual exploration or pedagogical pursuit. However, the limits on thesis length do not allow me to explore such insights thoroughly.

Secondly, although I have included 18 interviewees for more than half an hour in each individual interview, as well as revisits and checking through phone calls, attempts to generalize findings cannot be justified.

Thirdly, while inclusion of more informants generating a larger amount of data could give more credibility, rich data could result in many variables and much distraction, and analysis on individual cases in the depth could be affected, too. Also, data transcription and analysis proved to be extremely time-consuming. Therefore, it is suggested that future minor thesis should involve fewer participants and should further control variables to ensure deep and directional research.

Lastly, despite the fact that use of native language in interviews with the participants can facilitate full expression of their ideas and experiences, it has an obvious drawback: the essence of the original words and tone of the participants may sometimes be lost in the process of translation.

CHAPTER 4 RESULTS AND DISCUSSIONS

4.1 Introduction

This chapter examines the data collected from the interviews and analyses the participants' understandings of creativity and factors seen to foster and hinder the Chinese EFL major students' creativity from their interview data related to creativity and their campus life. The analysis and discussions are carried out according to the working model developed in Section 3.3 of Chapter Three. The purposes are to reveal the understandings of the EFL major participants about creativity as well as their possible relevant problems and to provide a basis for pedagogical implications related to changes in teaching policy.

Note that all the informants' names given in the analysis are pseudonyms.

4.2 Key Informants' Stories and Emerging Themes

In order to classify and evaluate the discussions more clearly, I chose two key informants from the 18 interviewees-a student, Xiao Yang (EES2) and a teacher, Yu Laoshi (EET1), whose interviews offered the richest insights. First, the stories told by each of these two key informants were analyzed according to the themes addressed in the semi-structured interviews. From their interview data, I categorized some creativity hindering/fostering factors and then extracted indicators of creative output and personal creative potential. These were then used as basic criteria for further study among all the participants in Sections 4.3 and 4.4 Section 4.5 summarizes this chapter.

4.2.1　Key Informant No 1: Xiao Yang

Xiao Yang (EES2) is an English major undergraduate in education, who has passed her Professional English Test Band 4 and is currently preparing for the National Band 8 test. In spite of all her hard work, she still lacks confidence in facing the Band 8 test. She also plans to take part in the postgraduate entrance examination, but has difficulty in choosing a major. She has been very fond of the English language ever since she began to learn English at middle school. English is so appealing to her that whenever she hears or sees English words or sentences, she automatically works to memorize these for future use. During the interview, she showed great interest in talking about creativity.

4.2.1.1　Creativity in and out of school

Xiao Yang mentioned that her memory is not particularly good. In order to keep up with the enormous amount of memorizing work required by all the English courses, she often resorts to "creativity" to assist her English learning. Asked to explain what she means when she says she resorts to creativity, she replied,

> You would find it a lot easier to memorize English words if you do it creatively using a little bit of your imagination. For example, I could never remember the name of a writer at first, but then I noticed that the first three letters are "ear" and somehow I connected this writer to this part of body and I never forget it anymore since then. There are always a lot of new words in the texts of the Advanced English course to us to recite. I created a method for myself: I would look up these new words in the dictionary first. After that, I would imagine some possible plots or stories and try to guess the rough meaning of the text with these words, then that's compared with the original text. Sometimes, what I imagined might just coincide with the meaning of the original text and I would become very excited. In this case, I would find it easy to understand the text and recite the words in it (p.5).

This quotation vividly describes how she has been using her memorizing schemes to compensate for her poor memory. The memory tricks, which she believes to be her own creative ideas or use of her "imagination", have greatly helped her English learning. She believes that everybody could be creating or using special language learning methods suitable for himself/herself. She wishes that such methods could be shared among students so that they would be able to "learn English more flexibly and less tediously".

Xiao Yang claims that native English speaking teachers' (called foreign teachers henceforth) lessons are beneficial for students' creative thinking because the foreign teachers always appreciate the students' innovative ideas. Unlike many Chinese teachers, foreign teachers are likely to appreciate individualized answers that are different from the key answers in a textbook.

In a business proposal, as required by her foreign composition teacher, Xiao Yang recalled that she noticed some professional hairstyle designers in business, and inspired by the extensive usage of computers, she creatively proposed that a computer could be used instead of manual design. A picture of the client could be taken and loaded into the computer and matched with various kinds of pre-loaded hairstyles. In this way, the customer would be able to personally see from the screen what he or she would look like with a particular hairstyle, and it would thus be a lot easier for him or her to choose the one that he or she was the most happy with. She added that the same idea could also be used in designing clothes to best fit customers' individual needs. She admitted she was not sure whether this idea is original, but she insisted that she did not copy anyone else, that is, this idea is subjectively original to her, and thus an example of her creativity.

In a short play she performed with her desk mate in a composition class as required by the same foreign teacher, they acted as a couple just before marriage. When she asked her "suitor" what else caused him to love her besides her beauty, he replied, "Your money", which stirred the class to laughter. She considered this answer a creative one because it is an unusual answer not expected by others. Then her "suitor" asked her what she would do if he were found out to be suffering from cancer after marriage, she said that she was seized by a sudden impulse and answered, "That's what I wish to see because you just love my money." She added that she had observed a lot of such "unexpected" remarks or jokes among her classmates that were quite "amazing", making people believe that he/she is creative to have thought of that. Xiao Yang also described some story-making activities that took place in the composition class,

> The teacher would give us several words with which we were supposed to make up a story. I think it's a very good way in cultivating our creative ability. Sometimes, he would give us the beginning of a story and asked us to carry on with the rest of the story. As a result, we always came up with different plots and various endings. If such activities had been organized more often, our creative ability and thinking would have been much improved now (p.6).

Xiao Yang (EES2) found her creativity most thoroughly expressed in her part-time work of coaching a grade-6 primary pupil in the English language,

> I would mime out the meaning of the words like "laugh" and "smile" for him to learn and review. Seeing that he likes drawing pictures, I would join him and ask him, "You know the Chinese for these things, don't you? Do you also want to know their English expressions?" He would then become very interested. I would write the English words on the pictures that he had drawn and teach him like that. After I taught him some simple imperative sentences for some times, I would tell him, "I'm your servant now. You can ask me to do anything you'd like by giving instructions in English." He became very excited and asked me to open the door, close the window and sweep the floor, etc. He learned quickly in this way (p.11).

This quotation shows that Xiao Yang was rather creative while she was working as a tutor. In retrospect, instead of being "uncreative" as she claimed, she did show great creative potential in creativity encouraging situations.

4.2.1.2 Creativity-hindering situations

Xiao Yang considers that many Chinese teachers, in contrast to foreign teachers, are "rather stiff" in teaching methodologies. Some of their Chinese teachers greatly depend on the standard key to the exercises in the textbooks to judge the students' answers,

> The teacher would be very positive to your answers that are exactly the same as the key attached to the textbook. For example, when you give a reply to a translation exercise, and if the teacher does not say anything, you would know that your answer does not accord the key and he or she is not satisfied with your answer. Then, the teacher would correct your answer according to the standard key (p.6).

Xiao Yang thinks that such an attitude is very harmful for the development of students' creative ability. "Instead of denying the students' answers in the first place", Xiao Yang said, "foreign teachers would confirm your different answers first, and then they will probably give you a more proper option. They appreciate your individualized answers and give you a lot of freedom" (p. 5, 6). The Chinese teachers' idea is that the students should "wait to be taught by teachers passively" while foreign teachers' concept is that the teachers ought to "enable the students to learn actively"; the Chinese teachers put emphasis on "mechanical memorization", and the foreign teachers focus on "communication" (p.6). Therefore, she considers foreign teachers' teaching to be beneficial for the development of students' creative ability.

She complained that she and her classmates have been constantly driven by tests, given no time to develop their thinking and creative ability,

> Tests, tests, everything is for tests, and everyday is for tests, from primary school to college. In order for their students to get through tests, teachers would put emphasis on memorization and belittle communication with students. They seldom stop and think how students' interest, creativity, and thinking ability could be elevated (p.6).

Xiao Yang thinks it very important to develop students' creative ability. In comparison with other majors, she thinks that English majors are less creative. She tends to impute the paucity of their thinking and creative ability mainly to excessive concentration on learning English,

> Most of us would only think of learning the English vocabulary, sentence structures and expressions in the texts...We are in such an environment every day. What we deal with is just reciting new words… We can't think much...We should pause a little from the blank daily words recitation and think about our future (p.9,10).

When asked how much she would seriously think about the ideas, viewpoints and the content involved in the English texts they learn, Xiao Yang replied that she rarely does so.

4.2.1.3 Future careers and creativity

As future English teachers, Xiao Yang believes that she and her classmates have to learn to teach creatively in order that their students might enjoy learning English.

> If you can only teach rigidly just like everyone else without any attractive features, you cannot hope that the students would be particularly fond of your English class...They will only like your class if your teaching is creative. It's also a must for the teacher to cultivate his/her students' creativity (p.9).

Xiao Yang told me that rather than use her English for teaching, she would like to work for a company "from the lowest level" when she graduates. To work in a company, she considers it very necessary for her to be creative:

> If you aren't creative, and if you can only work according to other people's instructions, maybe you will never be able to go up the ladders. However, if you can put forward your own ideas and suggestions, your success will be hopeful (p.9).

Xiao Yang seemed to be especially aware of the role of creativity in relation to the students' future careers. She was very appreciative that I brought up the topic of creativity with her. As she put it, "No one else has talked about creativity with me before, though I know it's extremely important for our future (p.12)."

4.2.1.4 Self-evaluation

Asked what she thought of the view that English majors are less creative than undergraduates of many other majors, Xiao Yang initially showed strong disagreement. However, as she carried on the conversation, she changed her ideas in an interesting way,

> No, I don't agree. I think people who study English are more open and active in thinking since they have more access for Western culture. I don't know if this has anything to do with creativity. I feel that students of English major are more confident than students of other majors (Her voice gradually weakened as she said this. She paused a little and continued). Maybe it's true that English majors are not so good as students of other majors in thinking and creative ability. I don't know even if we can think logically. Just like in the computer class we attended last Saturday, we could not think through some complicated issues. In fact, I had never thought of such issues in the past three years. This might be the reason that we are poorer in creative ability. English

majors are rather poor in logical thinking, unlike science students. If English majors are asked to do something that demands high creative ability and careful thinking, they are quite unlikely to be able to do that. I don't think they can ...Once, the computer teacher asked each of us to make a web page, I was so ashamed to see the colorful and creative work done by students from other institutes, while mine and several of my classmates' were so...(She blushed and stopped abruptly) (p.7).

The change of her attitude in the conversation suggests some psychological contradiction. I made some bold guesses about her thinking during the interview according to all the subtle clues I could detect. On the one hand, she could be thinking it necessary for her to stand up to argue for her peers and herself. However, when she carefully considered all the routine, it seemed that she could only think of mostly negative evidence. She hesitated about what she felt she had to say and what she wished to be able to say, but eventually decided to choose the former-to spell it out-although it was not easy to do that, as revealed through her pauses, hesitations, weakening tones, and blushing. I first noticed this shift of her attitude in reading the transcripts and began to wonder about the reasons for her doing so. Only when I went back to the tape did I find the subtler picture. Listening to the actual tape again helped me to recall the details I had noticed during the interview but had not thought were significant in gaining a deeper understanding of her behaviours, for example, her hesitations. This story also shows that she connects high-level creativity to very logical and careful thinking. In retrospect, I wondered if she senses that events such as her memory tricks and witty words are "small creativity" and need little logical, careful thinking.

In thinking about her postgraduate entrance examination, Xiao Yang (EES2) was quite lacking in confidence because of her poor content knowledge in any specific content domain and was at a loss as to what to major in for her postgraduate education,

> It's believed that English majors would have great privilege to win others at the examinations because of their high English level. I don't agree. Some time ago, I went to register for next year's postgraduate entrance examination, and at the office I came across some students from other institutes talking excitedly about their plans and so forth. I was quite embarrassed because I don't seem to know anything else except English. It's the big weak point of English majors to have learned nothing else but English. We know

little about psychology, science of education, mathematics and other courses. Our Chinese still remains at the level of high school students. What we have learned is too narrow. We've learned little in other respects, and our English is, maybe better than students of other majors, but still far from decent mastery. Isn't it a terrible failure for English majors? (p.8)

This quotation suggests that Xiao Yang is quite dissatisfied with her range of content knowledge, especially in comparison with students of other majors; she is also unsure if she, just like many other English major undergraduates, has really learned English well. She regards it as a great problem for the English majors.

Tourism English majors appear more knowledgeable than English Education majors as a whole, according to Xiao Yang, because of many content-based subjects they are required to study. Other than the normal TEFL courses, Xiao Yang noted that the inclusion of the curriculum units such as "On-the-spot Tour Guide" and "Tour Guide Basics" have structured a wide range of knowledge for the tourism English majors' communicative purposes and possible creative thinking.

Students of tourism English major are a lot better. Although they have not learned (English) grammar and basics in such details as we have, they are far better than us as far as routine communicative ability is concerned. To us English Education majors, it would be really difficult to talk about things such as hotel management, scenic places, and Chinese culture or ethnic cultures. But for the tourism English majors, it would be such a piece of cake. I have to say that they are better than us (p.10).

While Xiao Yang was showing little confidence in the English Education majors' creative ability, thinking ability, content knowledge, even in their English competence, she showed overwhelming admiration of her Tourism English major peers in these perspectives.

4.2.2 Key informant No. 2: Yu Laoshi

I chose Yu Laoshi as my study participant through recommendation of several of her students. Each of them, when asked to nominate a creative teacher in separate individual occasions, unanimously praised her highly and claimed her to be a creative and very effective teacher from whom they had learned a lot. Before that, I had also heard other people mention her being a very popular teacher. Because of her reputation as a "creative" teacher, I arranged an interview with Yu Laoshi.

Yu Laoshi teaches year-3 English majors Comprehensive English course, a key subject for English majors in China. This subject deals with grammar, speaking, listening, reading, writing, and translation, and prepares the students for national English Major Tests Band 4 and Band 8.

4.2.2.1 Why foster creativity?

Yu Laoshi insists that it is very important for the students to be creative,

> I dare say that creative ability is of vital significance for their future work. If you have an active thinking, you will be able to help your boss greatly. Also, you will have an outstanding ability in decision-making. The uncreative people are sure to be low in abilities. If you are very active and good in thinking, and active in mental activities, I think you would impress other people positively and would be very efficient in doing work. For teachers, creativity is even more important, because people you face are students; they need your directions. If teachers are conservative, lacking in liveliness and only knows how to follow prescribed instruction, their students would be most probably just like them in the future (p.44).

On one hand, this quotation indicates that Yu Laoshi highly values the importance of creativity for the sake of students' future work; on the other hand, it also shows her understanding of creativity. She used "active thinking", "active and good thinking", and "active in mental activities" as equivalents of "creativity" in opposition to "conservative", "lacking in vitality", and "following prescribed instruction". She seems to consider a creative person someone who can think actively and efficiently, and to regard an obedient person as uncreative.

Asked how creativity would affect the actual translation work that many English majors may undertake in their future career, Yu Laoshi points out,

> When involved in translation work, a person with active thinking will be able to deal with various urgent situations accordingly. He/she would be able to make sharp turns in language expressions and spit out something you would not be able to imagine (p.44).

She takes her husband as an example of showing creative thinking in translation,

> In many situations, I find that his thinking is different from us. While I might translate in one way, he would actually translate in a different and flexible way. He can judge the situations accurately according to different audiences and their varying preferences. He knows different people have different responses on hearing the same thing…He may not have the expertise at the relevant technological domain, but he is able to organize those things very flexibly according to the audience and the situation, express them in ways that the audience would understand…The expressions he uses cannot be typical professional jargons for they relate to some machinery equipments that he does not necessarily have access. But he is able to change a stance and translate them understandably (p.45).

Regarding written translation, she believes that the translator also needs to be creative and "active" in "thinking". She thinks that flexible personality makes a good interpreter, but a good piece of translation in written form is based more on the translator's wide range of knowledge.

Yu Laoshi (EET1) emphasized that the teachers should know how to enable their students to become aware of their own creative ability. While acknowledging that creative potentials could be inborn, she also admitted the importance of follow-up encouragement and development,

> For most people, I believe that their creative ability is in sound sleep waiting to be mined, developed, and encouraged. Teachers are obliged to do that for their students. The students should at least be made known that they possess an ability that they have never found themselves. If the teacher doesn't cultivate it, their creative gift may be deserted and lost forever. The key issue is how it can be cultivated (p.41).

To sum up, Yu Laoshi talked about all the advantages a creative EFL professional would have in relation to his/her EFL careers. She thinks that most people have creative ability but do not know about it. Therefore, it is important for the teacher to enable students to use and stretch their own creative ability so that this ability can be maintained and further cultivated.

4.2.2.2 Fundamental and advanced levels of EFL learning in relation to creativity

Starting from year-3, Yu Laoshi considers that the English majors should be guided towards more advanced language learning, rather than continuing further instruction in the basics of the language. She says,

> Having learnt English for 6 years at middle school plus 2 years of college study, altogether 8 years of English learning, their basic learning should be sufficient for a more advanced level. Fundamental English learning should no more take up a large part of their learning time. (p.30).

For EFL beginners, Yu Laoshi agrees that expression of their creative potential would be difficult, since they have to be led by teachers step by step or to fumble their own way through. However, as soon as they have completed this beginning process, everything should be different. She hopes that

> My students may surpass me. They ought to be perfect in their English expression, wide in content knowledge and rich in their thinking. I don't hope my students are rigid and take trust in whatever their teachers tell them... I hope that they have their own thinking, not just copy or follow others' ideas. They should have their own independent thinking (p.34).

4.2.2.3 Yu Laoshi's means of fostering creativity

The transition from the students' second year to the third year is crucial, according to Yu Laoshi, as it indicates that their study should transform from a primary level to a rather advanced level. However, many students cannot cope with the shift and they are not psychologically prepared for the change. Their learning style still conforms to an attitude where "teachers have all the say". They will do whatever the teacher asks them to do. "If the teacher has taught them one lesson, they would never learn two-very passive and obedient. They don't have their independent thinking (p.31)." In order to foster their independent thinking, Yu Laoshi thinks it essential to broaden their views and range of knowledge through the content revealed from the English texts. She describes what she does,

> In the first semester of the third year, I would ask the students to read something related to the content of texts they are learning so that their relevant knowledge is increased. For example, articles relating to religious issues, cultural differences, Sino-

Western cultural issues, including how African culture is influenced by the Western culture. I would infuse these into my teaching, and, I would give them such relevant articles to read after class. Sometimes, one lesson would take a long time to complete. In fact, most of the time is not spent to teach the superficial meaning of the text itself, but on the content beyond the text. For example, I used to teach them a lesson related to environment, just related, it's not strictly about environment. I changed the angle of seeing it and we involved the attitude of the British Government toward environmental protection…After that, the event was compared with the current American and Chinese situation. I just try such things with my efforts, to lead the students to think. (p.31)

In the second semester, Yu Laoshi would give the students something more difficult to read, works written by famous writers. Their textbooks contain selected famous works, but the selection or excerpts are often rather narrow and isolated. The students usually have difficulties in gaining a panoramic understanding about these writers' backgrounds and their works. Instead of just sticking to the selected parts in the textbook, Yu Laoshi requires the students to extend their reading to other works or complete versions of the works written by the authors, then write out their critical remarks about what they have read,

> I ask them to write about their remarks about the paragraphs, or sentences that have most impressed them. This helps them to develop their thinking and imagination and I think it has turned out to be rather effective. They do not have to follow their teacher's thinking. They are given a space for free imagination. When they return to the text, instead of being limited to what the text tells them, they would generally find their understanding a lot deeper and they are able to involve a much wider space in thinking. Therefore, it can do good to their thinking and imaginative ability. Then, after this stage, I would give them a complete piece of rather difficult original writing to read and ask them to write an essay about it. I would give them several choices. They could choose to write a commentary or critical journal about it… they are provided with bountiful room for free imagination…From my observation about my current students, I have observed a major progress in their thinking ability. What they can see is no more mere surface of the language, but something deeper inside (p.33).

Yu Laoshi admits that the current textbook has been a great problem for her because it still puts emphasis on basic language structures with a lot of grammatical and lexical exercises after each text. She always attempts to find a better way to incorporate the required textbook teaching with the cultivation of students' thinking and creative ability. She insists,

> I don't hope to see that my students can only understand what the textbook tells them. I hope to see in them very active thinking and imagination, see that they can fully express their ideas. Even if their ideas may be rather radical, or even wrong, their argument should be complimented as far as they can make it acceptable to others (p. 33).

Regarding the instances when students' answers are not in keeping with the exercise key, Xue Laoshi greatly encourages them to give answers different from the key. Their answers will be considered correct as far as the means of expression are acceptable.

According to Yu Laoshi, in order to foster students' creativity, it is necessary to provide them with subject content—the condition or context in which creative thinking can be applied. Therefore, instead of focusing solely on the language elements as in a traditional English course in China, she expands students' range of knowledge by referring to more information related to the texts and by assigning extra reading materials to the students. She mainly adopts journal writing as a means to check their understanding about the readings. Different views are encouraged. The kind of creativity she encourages in this respect sounds more like critical thinking and the methodology she adopts contains the most basic principles of content-based language instruction as discussed in section 2.4 of Chapter Two. Although she did not seem to be aware of content-based language instruction or related concepts, it appears she had been practicing it unknowingly but effectively.

4.2.2.4 Students' remarks about Yu Laoshi

> I think that Yu Laoshi's teaching method is very good, very suitable for us. For each lesson, she would not just teach us the text itself; she would surely add something else. For example, after having learnt an article about Irving, she would ask us to write a journal about it...After we had learned "Just 3 days to see", which is a very moving story, she asked us to write an article entitled "If I just had 3 days to see, I would..." Many of our classmates wrote wonderful stories...She often talked about interesting things she learned from elsewhere...The textbook is too old. Now another teacher came to teach

us the course and we soon become bored about her class. She just teaches everything according to the textbook, very meaningless, and very monotonous (p.87).

The above events described by Xiao Hang (EES3) further show Yu Laoshi's emphasis on content-teaching and involvement of students' independent thinking in promoting their interest. Xiao Niu (EES7) also states,

> When Yu Laoshi asked us to do translation exercise, we did not have to follow a fixed model. The summaries or journals about an article could all be written from our own stance...She gave us a lot of opportunities to express ourselves. To her, there's no such thing as "right" or "wrong". What she cares is your own ideas. Everyone is willing to show his/her opinions. There aren't many opportunities for us to show off ourselves at the college
> ...I particularly like the morning report (laughter). We can say anything we'd like to say. It's such a good time to tell other people what you think (laughter). If she taught us for another year, I would be willing to do morning report everyday (laughter) (p.95).

However, flexible teaching methods and content-based teaching do not seem to be sufficient to account for students' favour for Yu Laoshi's teaching, just as Xiao Hang puts it,

> Yu Laoshi gave us an outstanding feeling ever since she took over our "Comprehensive English" course. First of all, her professional ability is at a very high level and has an excellent temperament; she speaks good English. What moved us most is her dedication to teaching work. Once I asked her several questions at the end of my composition. She wrote a reply that ran even longer than my own composition...she wrote long comments to everyone. She checked so many exercise books sentence by sentence and word for word...Her seriousness enabled all of us to become serious. Everyone enjoys doing her assignments, though quite a lot, much is from outside the textbook such as meaningful paragraphs for us to translate...She would type out a good piece of translation or article written by the students and post it onto the walls for all of us to appreciate. She would often find the most well translated word or sentence and pay compliments to it with all of us, which has resulted in a heated competition among the students. Everyone wants to do well. Although she is not our master teacher, she gets along with us the most and the best. Unlike most college teachers, she would stay in the classroom after the class and chat with us. We are also willing to share our ideas with her (p.20, 21).

Xiao Niu (EES7) also offered similar remarks, but he added,

> The first time when she came to our classroom, we felt that her voice is very melodious, and felt as though she were a leader. We felt strongly overawed by her look of authority. Immediately, you feel that you have lagged behind too far much; it would never do if I don't work hard...When you feel lazy, she has all the power to kick you up from the seat and walk...We all wondered what is the real reason that enabled her to be able to move us forward while all the other teachers could not. It's hard to tell (laughter), really hard to tell (laughter)...(p.95)

This description seems to show that the students respect Yu Laoshi's teaching because of a number of combined factors: her impressive English competence, her serious attitude to teaching, her good relationship with the students, and her special personality. Xiao Hang highly evaluated the outcome of Yu Laoshi's teaching,

> She has just taught us for one year, but the academic atmosphere in the class becomes obviously better now and our overall English competence greatly enforced, speaking ability much improved. We had never expected such a big improvement before (p.21).

4.2.3 Themes emerging from key informants' stories

The stories told by Xiao Yang reveal that she has a constant interest in learning English. However, she does not seem to feel confident about herself in many ways. In the first place, she thinks that her range of knowledge is quite narrow in comparison with undergraduates of other majors. She also considers herself to be poor in thinking and creative ability. She does not even feel confident about her own English language competence. She tends to consider most of the English Education major undergraduates to be more or less like her. Even though tourism English majors share the same big umbrella of English major with the Educational undergraduates, she thinks that the former group is much better than the latter in content knowledge and flexibility.

Xiao Yang thinks it highly necessary for the students to be creative for the benefit of their future career. However, Xiao Yang complained that cultivation of this ability has never been taken seriously in the actual practice of the Chinese education, especially in the English major education. She imputes the students' paucity in creativity to be the result of their narrow range of knowledge, many tests, teacher-centeredness, teachers' discouraging different answers and highly mechanical English language learning process.

Most of the creative events she could recall took place in the composition class taught by a foreign teacher or in the assignments required by the teacher. She declared that in comparison with Chinese teachers' spoon-feeding lectures, foreign teachers' teaching methodology is more helpful in cultivating students' creative ability because they give the students free space to think and create. Her experience as a home tutor has also given her an opportunity to stretch her imagination and creative ability.

Yu Laoshi pays high regard to one's creative ability and believes that this ability will enable students to become competent teachers, interpreters, translators or business people. To her, creative ability is an inborn personal trait that many people have but are not aware of possessing. The teachers have the obligation to reveal or "draw out" the students' creative ability in order for them to strengthen their confidence and creativity. To foster students' creative potential, Yu Laoshi has implemented a series of teaching techniques that are in line with some basic ideas of content-based language instruction discussed in Section 2.4 of Chapter Two (Liu, 1999; Shih, 1999; Tang, 1997; Widdowson, 1990; Mohan, 1986). She agrees that TEFL at fundamental stage could be rather mechanical and involve much rote learning. However, she thinks that more advanced TEFL learners should focus more on the information shown through the language and should undertake more creative and independent thinking about content. Meanwhile, without giving up attention to the language elements altogether, Yu Laoshi seems to be adopting a teaching methodology that maintains balance between content and language. Her teaching appears to be quite fruitful in enhancing students' English language competence as well as in fostering the expression of their creative potential. From her students' stories, her special personality, her devotion to teaching work, her friendly and open attitude to students' different ideas all seem to be the basis of her success as a creative and effective teacher.

To sum up, from the two key informants' stories, the following factors are seen to hinder or foster expression of the EFL major students' creativity and these will be used as a basis to be compared across all the participants in the next section:

1. Factors seen to hinder the EFL major students' creativity: discouraging multiple answers, spoon-feeding teaching①, mechanical EFL learning process, test wash back, improper textbooks, and insufficient content knowledge.

2. Factors seen to foster the EFL major students' creativity: open-ended TEFL activities, student-centred teaching, communication between teacher and students, content teaching/learning, delightful/relaxed atmosphere, and extra-curricular activities.

  Yu Laoshi's stories and Xiao Yang's stories have also provided the following source indicators of creativity to be identified where present in all the 18 participants' interviews for comparison and analysis in Section 4.4:

1. Indicators of creative potential: flexibility, imagination, reflection, thinking ability, individuality/difference, interest/motivation, liveliness/activeness, independence, and good content knowledge.

2. Indicators of creative products: (work, ideas, or methods) useful/efficient, interesting, surprising/unexpected, special/different, and new/original.

Please note that terminology of the above factors and indicators have been modified in some cases to better categorize the meaning of those in the key informants' texts.

4.3 Factors Believed to Hinder/Foster Creativity

With the factors identified by the two key informants to be creativity hindering and creativity fostering, as discussed above, the occurrences of those in all the 18 participants' interview transcripts are noted. Some outstanding patterns are discussed below briefly.

---

① This refers to the traditional way of giving lectures where teachers try to force knowledge into the students' brains without considering students' active role in learning.

4.3.1 Factors seen to hinder EFL majors' creativity

Table 4-1 Factors seen to hinder EFL majors' creativity

	H1	H2	H3	H4	H5	H6
EES1		**	*			
EES2	*****	*****		***	**	**
EES3	****	**	****	**	***	*****
EES4	**	*	**		***	*
EES5	*	**	**		*	
EES6	**	*	*			
EES7	*	****	****	***** **	*****	*****
TES1	***		***	**		
TES2	**	*	**	*	*	
TES3	*	*	***	**		*
TES4	*	**	*	*	**	
EET1	****	**	***	***	*	*
EET2	**	***	*	**		*
TET1	****	***	*	***		
TET2	*	**				
TET3	**	**		*		
IA1	***	*				
IA2	*					
Total	39 times 17ps (94%)	34 times 16ps (89%)	28 times 13ps (72%)	27 times 11ps (61%)	18 times 8ps (44%)	16 times 7ps (39%)

Note: H1 = insufficient content knowledge; H2 = mechanical EFL learning process; H3 = improper textbooks; H4 = test wash back; H5 = discouraging multiple answers; H6 = spoon-feeding teaching.[1]

Factors that are seen to hinder the students' creativity include: insufficient content knowledge (as in the education students' worries about their poor content knowledge), mechanical EFL learning process (as in the monotonous recitation of English words), inappropriate textbooks (as in the out-of-fashion textbooks for

---

[1] Each " * " stands for one of the respective interviewee's references to each of these factors. The percentage stands for the ratio of the people who mentioned the topic in relation to the total population (ps = persons). EES: English Education Student; TES: Tourism English Student; EET: English Education Teacher; TET: Tourism English Teacher; IA: Institutional Administrator.

students' comprehensive English course), test wash back (as in the negative effects of the English band 4 or band 8 tests on the students' attitude to learning), discouraging multiple answers (like the use of the exercise key book as criteria to judge students' answers), and spoon-feeding teaching (like the traditional Chinese lecture-styled teaching).

As shown in the above table, while all the 6 factors have been frequently referred to, "insufficient content knowledge" (mentioned a total of 39 times by 94% of participants) and "mechanical TEFL learning processes" (mentioned a total of 34 times by 89% of participants) appear more frequently mentioned by the participants as factors believed to hinder the students' creativity. Two extracts from interviews further illustrate this sense of creativity-hindering factors. Asked how TEFL learning relates to creativity, Zhang Laoshi (EET2) admitted reluctantly,

> They are hard to relate to each other…The language itself cannot be created… as English is learned as a target language, the process of acquiring the language itself is short of creative elements. It doesn't require the learners to create. It is always better for the learners to recite as many new words as possible; they cannot create new words. Students of any other majors are given the free space to think but students of foreign language majors, who are restricted by their own major (p.50).

Xiao Hang's (EES4) perception of his inadequate content knowledge was highlighted when he went back home after the first semester to gather with his middle school classmates, who had been enrolled to study other majors elsewhere,

> We only separated for one semester, and we felt so different from each other as soon as we began to talk with each other. It seemed that they knew about everything and I knew absolutely nothing, just like an idiot. Just think about it, only a few months' separation (sighed and shook his head) (p.24).

4.3.2 Factors seen to foster the expression of EFL major students' creativity

Table 4-2 Factors seen to foster EFL major students' creativity

	F1	F2	F3	F4	F5	F6
EES1	**		*	**	*	*
EES2	***	***** *	****	***	*	**
EES3	***** **	**	*****	***** **	***** ***	****
EES4	*	*	*			*
EES5	**		***			
EES6	**	*	*			
EES7	***** ****	***	***** **	**	***** *****	*****
TES1	***	***	***	*	*	*
TES2	****	**	***			*
TES3	***	***	***	*		
TES4	****	*****	***			**
EET1	***** ***	***** **	***		*****	
EET2	**	***	*		*	*
TET1	*	*****	**	***		
TET2	*	*	*	**		
TET3	***	***	**	***		
IA1		**				
IA2		*		*		
Total	55 times 16ps (89%)	48 times 16ps (89%)	43 times 16ps (89%)	25 times 10ps (56%)	26 times 7ps (39%)	18 times 9ps (50%)

Note: F1 = open-ended TEFL activities; F2 = content teaching/learning; F3 = student-centred teaching; F4 = extracurricular activities; F5 = teacher-student communication; F6 = delightful/relaxed atmosphere.①

Factors that foster the students' creativity are believed to include "open-ended TEFL activities" (as in the foreign composition teacher's assignments and Yu Laoshi's translation exercises), content teaching or learning (as in the tourism English majors' content courses in Chinese), "student-centred teaching" (as in many of foreign

---

① Each " * " stands for one of the respective interviewee's references to each of these factors. The percentage stands for the ratio of the people who mentioned the topic in relation to the total population (ps = persons). EES: English Education Student; TES: Tourism English Student; EET: English Education Teacher; TET: Tourism English Teacher; IA: Institutional Administrator.

teachers' classroom activities), "extracurricular activities" (as in the poster-designing competition mentioned by Xiao Hang), "communication between teacher and students" (as in Yu Laoshi's good relationship with her students and their trust for her), and "relaxed atmosphere" (as in the delightful group work organized by the foreign teachers). Among these, "open-ended TEFL activities" (mentioned a total of 55 times by 89% of participants), "content teaching or learning" (mentioned a total of 48 times by 89% of participants), and "student-centred teaching" (mentioned a total of 43 times by 89% of participants) are most frequently referred to as factors beneficial to the expression of the EFL major undergraduates' creativity. Two further examples from students "stories" highlight their perception of creativity-fostering factors. Xiao Niu (EES7) recalled Yu Laoshi's open-ended content teaching thus:

> She would ask us to do translation without requiring us to do it in a unified model; she would also ask us to write comments or summaries on some articles or novels encouraging us to do them from our own aspects…So we almost always tried our best to express the essence our own ideas (p. 93).

In a simulated investment-attracting activity organized by a foreign teacher in which Xiao An (TES2) found herself quite creative, the teacher made up a big framework for the students to follow. He pretended to be an investor looking for a potential investment channel in tourism. The class was split up into several groups supposedly belonging to different travel companies looking for investment. He asked each group to design a special project and try to make it attractive to the investor. The students were asked to write an introduction for the proposed project in English and stick it to a bulletin board together with other designs and decors. At the presentation, each group of students had to explain their own project to the investor in the most attractive possible way and he would determine right at the spot the "company" he would like to invest on. Xiao An enthusiastically depicted her creativity in designing the project together with her group members:

I found and downloaded some pictures, then stuck them to a big piece of paper. By imagining an isle in the middle of the Pacific Ocean as our vacationing villa, each of our group members was supposed to introduce the range of business, capital and other conditions of the respective department of the villa that they were assumed to be responsible for. Before oral introduction to each department, a piece of music was played with a harmonica or a chorus was sung, and then some small acrobatics were performed. Very interesting, I must say.

4.4 Indicators of Creativity Across Participants

Based on the source indicators located from the two key informants of this study, this section examines the presence and frequency of these indicators in all 18 participants' interviews. Indicators of creative potential will be analysed first, and then indicators of creative product secondly.

4.4.1 Indicators of creative potential among participants

	A	B	C	D	E	F	G	H	I
EES1	*		*	***	***	***	*		
EES2	***** ***	***** ***** **	***** **	****	****	**** ***	****	****	****
EES3	***** ****	***	***** ****	*	**	***	**	****	*
EES4	***		*					*	
EES5	**	***	*						*
EES6	***		*	**	**	**	***	*	***
EES7	***** *	*****	***** ***	***** *	****	***	***	***	**
TES1	***	****		**		**	*		*
TES2	**	***		**		*			*
TES3	***** *	***** ***		*****	*	****	*		
TES4	*****	***** **		****	*	***			
EET1	***** ***** *	***** *****	***** ***** ***** ***** ***	***** *	***** **	**	***** *	****	***** *****
EET2	***	**	*					*	
TET1	***** **	***** ***** **	****	***** *****	****		**	***	*
TET2	**	*	**		*			**	
TET3	***	*	**	*			*****	*	
IA1	***	*		**	*				
IA2									
Total	77times 17ps (94%)	72times 15ps (83%)	66times 12ps (67%)	48times 13ps (72%)	30times 11ps (61%)	30times 10ps (56%)	28times 10ps (56%)	24times 10ps (56%)	24times 9ps (50%)

Note: A = good content knowledge; B = flexibility; C = thinking ability; D = independence; E = liveliness/ activeness; F = interest/motivation; G = individuality/difference; H = reflection; I = imagination.①

It can be seen from the above table that the most frequently mentioned indicators of creative potential among both students and teachers are "good content knowledge" (mentioned by 94% of participants for 77 times) and "flexibility" (mentioned by 83% of the participants 72 times).

Most English Education students seem to be quite worried about their insufficient content knowledge. Xiao Hang (EES3) insists that the paucity of their content knowledge has greatly narrowed their views and their creative thinking, and thus has affected their self-confidence as a whole. In comparing themselves with tourism English students, Xiao Hang sighed:

> As soon as they have learned tour guide speeches, they feel that they have learned a lot. But we have only been focusing on the English language. After having learned dozens of textbooks, we still feel that we've learned English and nothing in particular. Thus, we always feel that we know nothing. But tourism English students feel that they have learned a lot… Their information input is quite rich (p.19).

As a tourism English major student, however, Xiao An (TES2) also showed concern about her content knowledge limitation. She complained that the content knowledge they have learned from the textbooks is too limited and old and not sufficient to allow the flexibility to suit the various tastes of the tourists that she had guided in her spare time. Tong Laoshi (TET1) also points out that, "Our students (Tourism English majors) are rather short of creative ability academically. They should have learned the basics to carry out any real creative work (p.71)."

Many interviewees have mentioned "flexibility" almost as a synonym of "creativity". Xiao Wang (EES5) complimented foreign teachers for being more creative in that "They are more flexible in teaching styles (p.26)." In describing her creative teaching, Yu Laoshi emphasized the nature of "flexibility", "The teacher should be flexible to best suit the actual teaching process. I may need to change what I have prepared at any time according to the real situation (p.35)."

Also as shown in table 4 – 3, tourism students mentioned flexibility more frequently than education students. This concern might be related to their future career as tour guides. As Xiao Hang (EES3) claimed, "Their job is to consider how they can best draw their guests to them. This forces them to become very active in flexible thinking (p.17)." Sometimes, "flexibility" is referred to in its antonym form

---

① Each " * " stands for one of the respective interviewee's references to each of these indicators.

of "stiffness". For example, Xiao Yang told me her experience about learning computer and said that she always feels "quite stiff, very poor in creative ability (p. 8)."

It can also be noticed from table 4-3 that "thinking ability" (66 times by 67% of participants) is another frequently mentioned notion in relation to creativity. Most of the times, "thinking ability" is mentioned either in parallel with or in place of "creativity". This may indicate the participants' belief that "thinking ability" and "creativity" are closely related notions. It can also be noticed that the notion of "thinking ability" is especially frequently referred to by Yu Laoshi (28 times) and her two students Xiao Hang (9 times) and Xiao Niu (8 times). This might indicate that the Yu Laoshi and her students were much more aware of the importance of cultivating "thinking ability" than were other participants. This is a very significant avenue for further research, although it cannot be explored in depth in the present study.

4.4.2 Indicators of creative product

As shown in the below table, the most frequently mentioned indicator of creative products is being "useful or efficient" (mentioned 76 times and by all the informants). Also others frequently talked about being "special/different" (mentioned 54 times and by 89% of participants) and "own/independent" (mentioned 57 times and by 67% of interviewees). Much less mention was made of about creative products being "new/original" (only 7 times and by 17% of interviewees).

It seems that the participants consider a creative idea or work being "useful or efficient" as a very basic feature of creative product. For example, Xiao Hang (EES3) proudly talked about his poster design being creative as it proved to be very well received and attracted a lot of readers (p.17). However, he does not think some of Xiao Niu's surprising ideas creative, because they are "too radical and lopsided".

Section A TEFL and Beyond TEFL: Indicators of Creativity Among Chinese EFL Majors and Their Teachers

Table 4-4 Indicators of creative product seen by teachers and students

	O	P	Q	R	S	T
EES1	****	*		*	***	
EES2	*******	******	****	********	***	*
EES3	********	******	***			****
EES4	**	**	***			
EES5	***	***	**			
EES6	**	**	***		*	
EES7	********	*********	*********	****		
TES1	***		**	***		
TES2	**		*	****		
TES3	****		*	**		
TES4	***			***		
EET1	*****	**********	**********	******	*	
EET2	*****	***	**	**		
TET1	*****	*****	**			
TET2	**	**	***			
TET3	*******	******	***	*******		**
IA1	****		**			
IA2	**		*			
Total	76 times 18ps (100%)	57 times 12ps (67%)	54 times 16ps (89%)	40 times 10ps (56%)	8 times 4ps (22%)	7 times 3ps (17%)

Note: O = useful/efficient; P = own/independent; Q = special/different; R = interesting; S = surprising/unexpected; T = new/original.①

The majority of the interviewees highly value ideas or events that are created by the undertaker him/herself independently. Many of them emphasize the undertakers' subjective efforts and do not seem to worry much about whether or not the same idea or work have been undertaken by other people. For example, Xiao Mi (EES6)

---

① Each " * " stands for one of the respective interviewee's references to each of these factors. The percentage stands for the ratio of the people who mentioned the topic in relation to the total population (ps = persons). EES: English Education Student; TES: Tourism English Student; EET: English Education Teacher; TET: Tourism English Teacher; IA: Institutional Administrator.

described a typical creative event of this kind when she was studying at primary school. She had not been successful in her study by the time she entered grade four because she could not recite the texts well. However, as she was reading out a text aloud outdoors one day, she suddenly found that she was able to memorize the text much better than before. She tried the same thing again some more times and found it really efficient. Since then, she found an important rule about memory, i.e. reading aloud helps memorization. "I created a learning method," her eyes shone and she chattered on, "I read out everything I learn, Chinese, mathematics, and everything." It was obvious that this finding meant a lot to her because she soon became one of the best students in her class. "Of course, everybody seems to know this today", she argued, "but nobody ever told me about it then." She continued proudly, "To me, it was an original discovery. Maybe the most meaningful invention in my life, too (p.28)." When Yu Laoshi talked about encouraging students to express their own ideas, she did not seem to be particular about whether these ideas had to be really first-hand. What she cares for are ideas that have gone through the students' own subjective thinking process without consciously copying anyone else. The fact that most participants avoided using the terms "new" or "original" in relation to the creative ideas or event in their stories also seems to further indicate their intentional minimization of the original feature of creative products in their conception. Perhaps an appropriate label for such creativity would be "subjectively creative products", since they are a result of the personal endeavour of the undertaker, but have not been identified to be really new or original.

Many informants related creative ideas or events to being "special" or "different" from others in the specific environment. For instance, Xiao Hang (EES3) considers that the exhibits provided by him and his classmates were rather creative because they looked "so different from the rest of the exhibits" (p.14). As an English Education major undergraduate, Xiao Wang (EES5) thinks her idea of taking part in the "Tour Guide License Test" a creative one because no one else in her class thought of doing it (p.26). Perhaps such creative products would be better labelled "situationally creative products", since they are special in certain situations but do not have to be original in other settings. Such creative products would often include conscious adoption of ideas already put forward or practiced elsewhere, with adjustment of some kind to better suit the new situations. An example of this is Tong Laoshi's (TET1) suggestion that:

I don't think that creativity has to be necessarily something very different from anyone else's. As far as the students are able to effectively make use of other people's ideas to serve their own purposes, as far as they can utilize the relevant factors efficiently in the fulfilment of their aims, they can be considered to be creative, and quite creative, too (p.69).

4.5　Summary

Csikszentmihalyi (1994) suggests that creativity is a socially and culturally held concept that may vary according to different domains and fields. With this basic stance, the current study has examined Chinese EFL major students and their teachers' understanding about creativity, by adapting the initial working model developed in section 2.2.3 of Chapter Two and a final working model generated in Section 3.3 of Chapter Three. The initial working model suggests setting out the exploration of the participants' concept in creativity in two areas: creative potential (whether personal traits or thinking process), and creative product (whether "big" or "small"). The final working model suggests two layers of exploration through the inter-viewing data. The upper (or explicit) layer of the data provides immediate hints to factors that are seen to foster or hinder the TEFL major undergraduates' creativity. On the lower (or implicit) layer of the data, from how the teacher and student participants lay out their stories about creativity, indicators of creative product and personal creative potential are available to give insights about their understanding in creativity. These findings also function to inform pedagogical implications in the TEFL context of Chinese English majors.

This Chapter begins by recounting the interviews with two key informants. From these interviewees, emergent themes have been discussed; factors believed to be creativity hindering and creativity fostering have been elicited, and indicators of creativity (both creative product and personal creative potential) identified, which are then used as a basis for further comparison across all the participants. By attending to the occur-rences and frequencies of the factors and indicators, I have endeavoured to allow the voices of the two key informants to be heard and, more briefly, the voices of other informants. From these voices, certain recurrent patterns emerge.

The Chinese EFL majors and their teachers tend to believe that "mechanical TEFL learning processes" and "insufficient content knowledge" are the key reasons that affect the expression of EFL major, especially English Education major students' creativity. The participants are also inclined to believe that "open-ended TEFL activities", "student-centred teaching" and "content teaching or learning" can greatly help to foster the expression of students' creativity.

The Chinese EFL major participants are apt to talk about creative persons being "flexible" and "knowledgeable", and creative products (ideas, events or activities) being "useful/efficient" and "own/independent". Meanwhile, they tend to minimize the "new or original" feature of the creative products. All these indicate that the English major participants do value creative potential that helps to yield "situationally creative products" and "subjectively creative products".

CHAPTER 5   SUMMARY AND CONCLUSIONS

5.1   Introduction

The research questions of this study as posed in Chapter Two are:

1. What are the indicators of creativity (creative product and creative potential) according to the English language and literature major undergraduates and teachers interviewed?

2. According to EFL major participants, what are the factors that hinder or foster TEFL majors' creativity present in the current English major program?

3. What implications can be drawn for Chinese EFL major education to foster the students' creativity in their TEFL courses?

In order to provide answers to each of these research questions, this chapter summarizes the major findings of the study. Then limitations of this study are noted, and some possible directions for further research suggested.

5.2   Factors Seen to Hinder/Foster EFL Majors' Creativity

Many TEFL major participants believe that the factors that hinder TEFL major students' creativity include "students insufficient knowledge, "mechanical EFL learning process", "improper textbooks", "test wash back", the "teacher discouraging multiple answers", and "spoon-feeding teaching methods". The first two of these the students" "insufficient knowledge" and "mechanical EFL learning processes" seem to be their greatest concerns. In order to master the English language and pass the English Major Tests (band 4 and/or band 8), many students devote most of their time and energy to mechanical means of learning the language. Such learning experiences restrict students' opportunities to develop their creative ability. Moreover, the process of teaching and learning English generally does not involve much content learning, so that students lack a content environment in which to use language to explore ideas in any depth. This is especially true of English Education majors. Their comparative poverty of content knowledge is seen not only to hinder their creativity, but also to affect their self-confidence in relations to their peers in other more content-based major studies.

Factors that foster the students' creativity are thought to include "open-ended TEFL activities", "student-centred teaching", "communication between teacher and students", "relaxed atmosphere", "extracurricular activities", and "content teaching or learning". In order of listing, the first three factors above-"open-ended TEFL activities", "student-centred teaching", and "content teaching or learning" are the most frequently mentioned as beneficial to the cultivation of the EFL major undergraduates' creativity. Yu Laoshi's open-mindedness to students, as well as her lessons in which content knowledge is merged with TEFL teaching are high-lighted as creativity fostering. Some foreign teachers' classroom activities or assignments are also noted to be creativity fostering TEFL methods.

5.3 Indicators of Creative Potential and Creative Product

Indicators of creative potential identified by the Chinese TEFL major students and teachers include "good knowledge", "flexibility", "thinking ability", "independence" "liveliness or activeness", "interest or motivation", "individuality or difference", "reflection", and "imagination". The first two of these— "good knowledge" and "flexibility" appear to be the most significant indicators in relation to their understanding about creative potential, as highlighted in comments on tourism English major students.

Indicators of creative products identified by the Chinese EFL major students and teachers include work, ideas, or methods that are "useful and efficient", "own or independent", "special or different", "interesting", "surprising or unexpected", and "new or original". Among these indicators, the participants tend to refer to the "useful or efficient", "own or independent", and "special or different" features of creative products the most, and do not seem to regard "new or original" features as their major concern. The participants' lack of emphasis on the "new or original" characteristics is not in keeping with the basic novel feature of creative products as defined by most researchers (Mayer, 1999). This highlights the Chinese EFL major participants' preference for talking about creative products that are special or different in a certain situation, and those that are undertaken independently without consciously copying anyone else. These two types of creative product might thus be termed "situationally creative product" (product that is different or special in a certain situation, but not necessarily in some other situations) and "subjectively creative product" (product that is yielded with the undertaker's own or independent efforts, whether or not it is an unwitting repetition of other creative products).

Analysis of the data in this research tend to indicate that the pattern shown in these frequently mentioned creative products represents a professionally held concept of creativity in the Chinese EFL major field. Though this study does not permit generalization owing to the limited number of participants, as discussed in Chapter Three, its results do show the TEFL participants' obvious enthusiasm about creative products that are situationally or subjectively creative. Clearly, these are different from "big" creativity that forms the core of Csikszentmihalyi's DIFI model.

Meanwhile, "flexibility" and "good content knowledge", the features of personal creative potential most frequently mentioned by the EFL major participants, seem more likely to bring out creative products at a more humble level in routine practices, than to yield "big" creativity. Of particular interest here is the way the participants' concepts about creative product and creative potential seem to be merging together. While the participants see "big" creativity as rather distant from their real lives and their practical EFL careers, they obviously consider "small" creativity to be ordinary but much more accessible to them. The creative potential that directly helps to yield "small" creative product also seems to be less extraordinary but more accessible to them. The findings show the obvious enthusiasm of the EFL major participants about "small" creativity and their awareness of the significant part "small creativity" plays in fostering the students' creative potential, overall.

The findings point to intriguing new questions. As "small" creativity seems to be more appealing and of more practical value to wider populations in the EFL careers, why should research in this area be neglected? And since the DIFI model is not as applicable, how should research in "small" creativity be framed and carried out more systematically?

5.4 Pedagogical Implications

The interview data show that the traditional Chinese EFL major program is seen by both teacher and student participants in this study to present critical drawbacks in terms of fostering creativity, and support the view that the current programs are "high in investment but low in production" (Zeng, 2000; Li & Liu, 2001). An overall picture of interviews reflects the EFL major informants' pervasive diffidence in the English Education majors' creative and thinking abilities, content knowledge, and their English language competence. After having spent several years studying the English language constantly, many English Education majors still find their English competence quite low; others may have good English competence, but are believed to be very narrow in their range of knowledge, poor in thinking and creative ability. The results have further confirmed some Chinese TEFL educators' comments about the EFL majors in China (Liu, 1999; He, Yin, Huang & Liu, 1999; Liu, 2000; Zeng, 2000; Li & Liu, 2001).

Some foreign teachers' teaching has been found to be quite creative and creativity encouraging. They tend to organize TEFL activities and give assignments to the students that are more open-ended than are those given by many Chinese teachers. The students' preference for such tasks is obvious.

Although this study was not intended to compare English Education majors and Tourism English majors, a perception that emerged in the interviews is that Tourism English majors are better than English Education majors in "flexibility" and "content knowledge". This result is believed to be closely related to the content of the courses the Tourism English majors take in tourism domain while English Education majors do not. Tourism English majors are also thought to be generally more "flexible" (or more creative) than English Education majors.

The tourism English major program seems rather efficient in expanding students' range of knowledge in a certain domain and in increasing their creative potential. However, time devoted to learning the English language has been reduced since most of these content courses are only taught in Chinese. A model EFL major program seems to reside in integrating content teaching into TEFL courses by adopting content-based language instruction.

Content-based TEFL is especially suitable for advanced learners (Shih, 1999; Liu, 1999), since it helps to teach them how to use the language to learn (Mohan, 1986), and to improve their English language competence (Widdowson, 1968, 1978, 1990).

However, in the Chinese TEFL major program, the addition of content-based language instruction necessitates that teachers adjust their teaching so that both content and the English language can receive balanced attention in TEFL classes, as shown in Yu Laoshi's practices. Yu Laoshi assigns her students to do after-class readings and to write reflective journals in response to the readings. The students are asked to discuss subject matter and write their reflections on issues related to the texts. While expanding greatly on the content information of the texts, she has maintained some traditional exercises focusing on language. She asks her students to do translation, too, but selects only the difficult sentences or paragraphs from the texts that would directly affect their understanding of the content. Yu Laoshi's most favourite assignments also include her selection of some meaningful paragraphs beyond the textbook for the students to translate. In other words, the successful teaching methodology Yu Laoshi has adopted is more than just content-based teaching instruction. She has placed dual emphasis on content and language elements, and has mixed traditional pedagogy into modern TEFL ideology, to suit the practical Chinese TEFL situation.

Yet, Yu Laoshi's balanced and special methods alone do not seem to be sufficient to explain her fruitful teaching outcome. Her students sound particularly impressed by the high quality of her English, her devotion to teaching, and her personality, especially her friendliness and open-mindedness. All these have become good reasons for the students to pay high respect to her and to work hard to achieve success in their study. She seems to embody a combination of Chinese traditional and modern ideologies—she is open-minded and friendly to her students while maintaining her authoritative image and high respect from the students.

All these special features of Yu Laoshi's teaching methodology, ideology, and personality contribute to her students' identification of her as a creative teacher. Yu Laoshi represents one model for generating an intellectual and social environment that is likely to foster the development of creativity and students' English language competence through both pedagogical strategies and teacher-student relationship. Undoubtedly, there are other models, but in this study, Yu Laoshi's model has emerged to be particularly enlightening in this Chinese EFL context.

5.5 Proposal for Future Research

Many interesting issues have emerged in the current study.

First of all, this study suggests that Tourism English majors are believed to be more "creative" and "knowledgeable" than English Education majors even though both groups are under the same umbrella of English Language and Literature major, study almost the same TEFL textbooks and experience similar teaching methodologies. A quantitative study with a large number of students of these two groups would produce an interesting comparison between the two sub-majors. A deeper longitudinal qualitative study between these two groups of students could also contribute to richer insights in understanding this phenomenon.

Secondly, given more time, models such as Yu Laoshi's teaching methods in the TEFL course could have been more thoroughly studied by means of classroom observation and through her life story. Such a study may obtain some significant insights in helping to guide a more practical introduction of content-based language instruction in the Chinese TEFL context.

Thirdly, if the English Syllabus designers were accessible, it would be a meaningful study to compare their concepts of creativity with the concepts held by the teachers and students of English major program, the actual implementers of the Syllabus. A definition of creativity in the English syllabus may be necessary, so that the role of creativity in the EFL major field is explicitly and richly defined.

Fourthly, given more time for data gathering, the role of critical thinking in relation to the topic of creativity, could have been explored in greater depth. It would certainly be most enlightening to link them together in TEFL discussion in a longer thesis.

Lastly, as discussed in Section 5.2, the research on "small" creativity in the Chinese EFL major field cannot be neglected since it is more appealing and is of more practical value to wider populations. As the DIFI model is not as applicable, future researches in "small" creativity need to be framed so that they can be carried out more systematically. This study has provided starting points from where more substantial studies may follow in order to foster, document and understand "small" creativity in EFL context.

References:

Amabile, T. M. Growing up creative. Buffalo, NY: The Creative Education Foundation, 1989.

Anderson, H. Creativity as Personality Development. In Harold H. Anderson (Ed.), Creativity and its Cultivation. New York: Harper and Row, 1959.

Balkan, L. Les effects du bilinguisme francaise-anglais sur les aptitudes intellectuelles. Bruxelles: Aimav, 1970.

Bastid, M. Servitude or liberation? The introduction of foreign educational practices and systems to China from 1840 to the present. In R. Hayhoe & M. Bastid (Eds.), China's Education and the industrialised world: Studies in cultural transfer: 3-20. New York. London: M. E. Sharpe, Inc, 1987.

Beifang Ketizhu. Thinking on the Educational Reform of Foreign Language Majors. Foreign Language Teaching and Research, 1998, 115/3: 5-9.

Bell, J. Doing your research project: A guide for first-time researcher in education and social science. Philadelphia: Open University Press, 1987.

Ben-Zeev, S. The influence of bilingualism on cognitive development and cognitive strategy. Unpublished Ph. D. dissertation. University of Chicago, 1972.

Besemer, S. P., & O'Quin, K. Creative product analysis: Testing a model by developing a judging instrument. In S. G. Isaksen (Ed.). Frontiers of creativity research: Beyond the basics, 1987: 367-389. Buffalo, NY: Bearly.

Bogdan, R., & Biklen, S. K. Qualitative research for education: An introduction to theory and methods. Boston: Allyn and Bacon, 1982.

Braine, G. Comments on Ruth Spack's "Initiating ESL students into the academic discourse community: How far should we go?" TESOL Quarterly, 1982(22/4): 700-702.

Brick, J. China: A handbook in intercultural communication. Sydney: National

Centre for English Language Teaching and Research, Macquarie University, 1991.

Brinton, D. M., Snow, M. A., & Wesche, M. B. Content-based second language instruction. New York：Newbury House, 1989.

Burnaby, B., & Sun, Y. L. Chinese teachers' views of Western language teaching：Contextinforms paradigms. TESOL Quarterly. 1989(23/2)：219-238.

Burns, R. B. Introduction to research methods. Melbourne：Longman, 1994.

Byron, S., & Macmillan, M. The role of language teachers in distance education. In Y. F. Dzau (Ed.), English in China, 1990：193-201. Hong Kong：API Press Ltd.

Byron, S., & Macmillan, M. The role of language teachers in distance education. In Y. F. Dzau (Ed.), English in China, 1990：193-201. Hong Kong：API Press Ltd.

Chen, Z. L. . Intellectual economy and development. China's Scholars Abroad, 1998(8)：3-4.

Cortazzi, M., & Jin, L. X. Cultures of learning：Language classrooms in China. In H. Coleman (Ed.), Society and the language classroom, 1996：169-206. Melbourne：Cambridge University Press.

Craig, B. A. Boundary discourse and the authority of knowledge in the second-language classroom：A social-constructionist approach. In J. E. Alatis et al., (Eds.), Georgetown University round table on languages and linguistic, 1995：40-54. Washington D.C.：Georgetown University Press.

Csikszentmihalyi, M. The Domain of Creativity. In Feldman, D. H., Csikszentmihalyi, M., & Gardner H. (Eds.), Changing the World：A Framework for the Study of Creativity, 1994：135-158. Westport, Connecticut, London：Praeger.

Csikszentmihalyi, M., and R. Robinson . Society, culture, and person：A systems view of creativity. In R. J. Sternberg (ed.), The nature of creativity, 1988：325-339. New York：Cambridge University Press.

Cropley, A. J. Fostering creativity in the classroom：General principles. In M. A. Runco. (Ed.) Creativity research handbook, 1997(1)：83-114. Cresskill, N. J.：Hampton Press.

Cummins, J., & M. Gulutsan . Some effects of bilingualism on cognitive functioning. In：Bilingualism, biculturalism, and education. Edited by S. Carey. Edmonton：Universtity of Alberta Press, 1974.

De Avila, E., & S. Duncan . Bilingualism and the metaset. NABE Journal,

1979(3):1-20.

Denzin, N. & Lincoln Y. Handbook of Qualitative Research (2nd ed.)2000:1-28. Thousand Oaks, C. A.

Diesing, P. Patterns of discovery in the social sciences. New York: Aldine,1971.

Doolittle, J. H. Creative Reasoning Test. Pacific Grove, CA: Midwest Publications/Critical Thinking Press,1990.

Dudek, S. Z., Strobel, M. G., & Runco, M. A. Cumulative and proximal influences on the social environment and children's potential. The Journal of Genetic Psychology, 1993(154 /4):487-499.

Feldman, D. H., Csikszentmihalyi, M., & Gardner H. A Framework for the Study of Creativity. In Feldman, D. H., Csikszentmihalyi, M., & Gardner H. (Eds.), Changing the World:A Framework for the Study of Creativity,1994:1-45. Westport, Connecticut, London:Praeger.

Fleith, Denise de Souza . Teacher and student perceptions of creativity in the classroom environment. Roeper Review, 2000(22/3):148-157.

Flowerdew, J., & Miller, L. On the notion of culture in L2 lectures. TESOL Quarterly,1995(29/2):345-373.

Fontana, A. and Frey, J. H. The interview: From Structured Questions to Negotiated Text. In N, K. Denzin and Y. S. Lincoln (Eds.), Handbook of Qualitative Research,2000:645-672. London:Sage Publications, Inc.

Ford, D. J. The twain shall meet: the current study of English in China. Jefferson, North Carolina and London: McFarland & Company, Inc., Publishers,1988.

Gao, B. Q. A comparative study of teacher-student relations in the period of modernisation: China and the West. Unpublished PhD dissertation, La Trobe University, Melbourne,1993.

Gaoden Xuexiao Waiyu Zhuangye Jiaoxue Zhidao Weiyuanhui Yingyuzu . Teaching Syllabus for English Major of Higher Education: 12. Shanghai Foreign Language Education Press & Foreign Language Teaching and Research Press,2000.

Gedo, J. E. The creativity of women. Annual of Psychoanalysis,2000(28):215-223.

Georghiades, P. Beyond conceptual change learning in science education: focusing on transfer, durability and metacognition. Educational Research,2000(42/

2):119-139.

Glasersfeld, E. V. Introduction: Aspects of Constructivism. Constructivism: Theory, Perspectives, and Practice, 1996 Chapter 1:2.

Glesne, C., & **Peshkin**, A. Finding Your Story: Data Analysis. In C. Glasne and A. Peshkin (Eds.) Becoming Qualitative Researchers: An Introduction (Chapter 7). NY: Longman, 1992.

Grant, A. A Multi-storied Approach to the Analysis: Narrative, Literacy and Discourse. Melbourne Studies in Education, 1997(38/1):35-46.

Guba, E. G. & **Lincoln**, Y. S. Fourth Generation and Evaluation. Sage Publications, 1989.

Guilford, J.P. Creativity. American Psychologist, 1950(5):444-454.

Guilford, J. P. The Nature of Human Intelligence. New York, McGraw-Hill Book Co, 1967.

Harvey, P. A Lesson to be learned: Chinese approaches to language learning. ELT Journal, 1985(39/3):183-186.

He Qixin, **Yin Tongsheng**, **Huang Yuanshen**, **Liu Haiping**. Some ideas about educational reform on foreign language BA major. Foreign Language Teaching & Researches, 1999(117/1):24-28

Hitchcock, G., & **Hughes**, D. Research and the teacher. A qualitative introduction to school-based research. London: Routledge, 1989.

Hjelle, L. A. and **Ziegler**, D. J. Personality. New York: McGraw-Hill Book Company, 1976.

Ho, J., & **Crookall**, D. Breaking with Chinese cultural traditions: Learner autonomy in English language teaching. System, 1995(23/2):235-243.

Hu, C. D. English pedagogy. Beijing: Higher Education Press, 1994.

Ianco-Worrall, A. Bilingualism and cognitive development. Child Development, 1972(43):1390-1400.

Koh A. Towards a critical pedagogy: creating "thinking schools" in Singapore. Journal of Curriculum Studies, 2002(34/3):255-264. Taylor & Francis Group.

Kramer-Dahl, A. Critical reflexivity and the teaching of teachers of English. Discourse: studies in the Cultural Politics of Education, 1997(18/2):259-277.

Krashen, S. Principles and Practice in Second Language Acquisition. New York: Prentice Hallm, 1982.

Krashen, S. The Input Hypothesis. Beverly Hills, CA: Laredo Publishing

Company, 1985.

Krashen, S. and Terrell, E. The Natural Approach. Language Acquisition in the Classroom. Oxford:Pergamon, 1983.

Kumar, V. K., Kemmler, D., & Holman, E. R. The Creativity Styles Questionnair-Revised. Creativity Research Journal, 1997(10):51-58.

Landry, R. G. The Enhancement of Figural Creativity Through Second Language Learning at the Elementary School Level. Foreign Language Annals, 1973(7):111-115.

Larsen-Freeman, D., & Long, M. H. . An introduction to second language acquisition research. London:Longman, 1991.

Lazaraton, A. Qualitative research in applied linguistics: A progress report. TESOL Quarterly, 1995(29/3):455-472.

Leininger, M. Evaluation criteria and critique of qualitative research students. In J. M. Morse (Ed.) Critical Issues in Qualitative Research Methods: 95-115. Thousand Oaks. London. New Delhi:SAGE Publication, 1994.

Li, X., & Walker, K. Autonomy and accountability in higher education: An analysis of Chinese higher education reform. Canadian and International Education, 1997(26/2):9-27.

Li, Yi & Liu Shicong . Enforcing quality education as a means of solving problem of "high investment and low production" in foreign language teaching. Foreign Languages and Their Teaching, 2001(150/10):43-62.

Liebman-Kleine, J. In defense of teaching process in ESL composition. TESOL Quarterly, 1988(20/4):783-788.

Liu, Runqing . Trend of development in foreign language teaching and research. Foreign Language Teaching & Reaserch, 1999(117/1):7-12

Liu, Yi . Course Construction for Foreign Language Majors of Higher Education. Waiyujie (Foreign Language Field), 2000(3):12

Lofl and, J. Analysing social settings. New York:Wadsworth, 1971.

Maslow, A. Motivation and Personality (2nd edition). New York:Harper and Row, 1970.

Maley, A. XANADU—A miracle of rare device: the teaching of English in China. In J. M. Valdes (Ed.), Culture bound:Bridging the cultural gap in language teaching, 1986:102-111. Cambridge:Cambridge University Press.

Mayer, R. E. "Fifty years of creativity research", in Sternberg, R. J. (Ed.),

Handbook of creativity. Cambridge University Press, Cambridge, 1999:449-460.

Mohan, **B. A.** Language and content. Reading, MA:Addison-Wesley,1986.

Murphy, **J. M. & Stoller**, **F. L.** Sustained-content language teaching: an emerging definition. TESOL Journal, Autumn,2001:3-6.

Nanfang Zhu. Suggestions on the Educational Reform of Foreign Language Majors. Foreign Language Field,1998(71/3):1-4.

Orton, **J. M.** Educating the reflective practitioner in China: a case study in teacher education. Unpublished doctoral dissertation, La Trobe University, Melbourne,1990.

Paine, **L. W.** The teacher as virtuoso: A Chinese model for teaching. Teachers College Record,1990(92/1),49-81.

Paine, **L. W.** Teaching and modernisation in contemporary China. In 18. Hayhoe (Ed.), Education and modernisation: the Chinese experience, 1992: 183-209. Oxford:Pergamon Press.

Pally, **M.** Critical thinking in ESL: an argument for sustained content. Journal of second language writing,1997(6/3):293-311.

Patton, **M. Q.** Qualitative Interviewing. Qualitative Evaluation and Research Methods (2nd ed. Chapter 7). Newbury Park, CA:Sage;1990.

Pennycook, **A.** The cultural politics of English as an international language. Essex, England:Longman,1994.

Porter, **E. A.** Foreign teachers in China: Old problems for a new generation, 1979-1989.New York. London:Greenwood Press,1990.

Reid, **J.** Comments on Vivian Zamel's The composition processes of advanced ESL students: Six case studies. TESOL Quaterly, 1984(18/1):149-159.

Ren, **Jianxiong**. Functions of Higher Education and Creativity. Lilun qianyan (Frontline of Theories),2001(2):17-18.

Rosen, **H.** Troublesome Boy, London, English and Media Centre,1993:149

Ross, **H.** China learns English: language teaching and social change in the People's Republic. New Haven and London:Yale University Press,1993.

Selltiz, **C.**, **Jahoda**, **M.**, **Deutsch**, **M.**, **& Cook**, **S. W.** Research methods in social relations. London:Methuen,1965.

Shih, **M.** More than practicing language: Communicative reading and writing for Asian settings. TESOL Journal,1999(8/4):20-25.

Soh, **K.**, **C.** Indexing Creativity Fostering Teacher Behavior: A Preliminary

Validation Study. Journal of Creative Behavior, 2000(34/2):118-134.

Spanos, G. On the integration of language and content instruction. Annual Review of Applied Linguistics, 1987(10):227-240.

Sternberg, R. J., & Williams, W. M. How to develop student creativity. Alexandria, VA:Association for Supervision and Curriculum Development,1996.

Sun, Z., & Wu, J. Pedagogy. Changchun:Jilin Education Press,1986.

Szalay, L. B, Stroll, J., Liu, F., & Lao, P. S. American and Chinese perceptions and belief systems:a People's Republic of China-Taiwanese comparison. New York and London:Plenum Press,1994.

Tang, G. M. Teaching Content Knowledge and ESL in Multicultural Classrooms. In M.A. Snow & D.M. Brinton (Ed.), The Content-based classroom: Perspectives on integrating language content,1997:69. White Plains:NY Longman.

Tardiff, T. Z., & Sternberg, R. J. What do we know about creativity? In R. J. Sternberg (Ed.), The nature of creativity,1988:429-440. New York:Cambridge University Press.

Taylor, C. W., & Ellison, R. L. The Alpha Biographical Inventory. Greensboro, NC:Prediction Press,1968.

Ting, Y. R. Foreign language teaching in China:Problems and perspectives. Canadian International Education,1987(16/1):48-61.

Torrance, E. P. Guiding creative talent. Englewood Cliffs, NJ:Prentice-Hall,1962.

Torrance, E.P. Creativity. Association of Classroom Teachers of the National Education Association. San Rafael, Calif:Dimensions Pub. Co,1983.

Torrance, E. P. Torrance Test of Creative Thinking:Norms and technical manual. Beaconville, IL:Scholastic Testing Services,1999.

Tuckman, B. W. Conducting educational research. New York:Harcourt Brace Jovanovich,1972.

Urban, K. K., & Jellen, H. G. Test for Creative Thinking-Drawing Production (TCT-DP). Lisse, Netherlands:Swets and Zeitlinger,1996.

Wan, D. H. In People's Daily (Overseas edition), 2 February, 1999:7.

Wang, Y. B. On Cultural Blocks to Creativity in Chinese Society. Thesis submitted in partial fulfilment of the requirement for the degree of master of Education, School of Education, La Trobe University,1988.

White, M. Re-authoring lives:Interview and essays. Adelaide:Dulwich Certure

Publications, 1995.

Widdowson, H. The teaching of English through science. In J. Dakin, B. Tiffen & H. G. Widdowsn (Eds.), Language in Education: The problems in Common wealth Africa and The Indo-Pakistan sub-continent. London: Oxford University Press, 1968.

Widdowson, H. Teaching language as communication. London: Oxford University Press, 1978.

Widdowson, H. Aspects of language teaching. Cambridge, MA: MIT Press, 1990.

Yin, K. Case study research: Design and methods (revised edition). London: Sage, 1989.

Yu, C. C. Cultural principles underlying English teaching in China. Language Learning and Communication, 1984(3/1):29-40.

Zeng, Lisha On Enhancing Dialectic Thinking in Disciplines and Developing More Innovative and Creative Graduates. Journal of Shaoyang Teachers College, 2000(22/4):85-88

Zhang, Z. D., Huang, T. Q., & Yang, Z. C. A course in English language teaching methodology for students of higher normal schools. Chengdu: Electronic Science Press, 1993.

Appendix I
Questions for Semi-Structured Interview

I. **Proposed Questions for interview with undergraduates of English major**

1. Would you please describe for me one of your recent days at school that stands out in your memory?

2. What do you hope to achieve through your study as an English major? Have there been any changes since your entrance? What are they if any and why?

3. In your classroom, what kinds of students are most favored/admired by the teachers? What kinds of students are most favored/admired by the students?

4. In your opinion, whom would you think of as "creative people"? In what ways are they creative?

5. (If they only mention about well-known people) Have you observed any people doing creative things/being creative in your class or among people you know personally? How can you tell that they are creative? What would show you? What kind of people are they?

6. Do your teachers or classmates appreciate the creative students? In what ways?

7. Can you tell me a story where you observed creative thinking or activities had taken place in your English class? How did it impress you?

8. Have you ever thought or acted creatively? Would you mind telling me the story in detail?

9. In which courses is creativity most involved? How? What do you think of the involvement?

10. In which courses is creativity not so relevant? How do you like the course(s)?

11. As far as you can see, are there any differences between Chinese and foreign EFL teachers regarding their attitudes toward expressions of different opinions? How do their attitude to different opinions influence your creative thinking?

12. What do you wish your teachers would or would not do in English lessons? How much do you think it necessary/unnecessary for the teachers to be creative?

13. Would you tell me something about a creative English teacher you know?

14. How do you find your future work/life has to do with creativity?

II. Proposed Questions for interview with Chinese teachers of English major

15. What difficulties/puzzles have you come across in teaching your current English majors (if any)? In what ways do they affect your teaching and students' learning?

16. What do you hope for in your graduating English majors? Has there been any change in your hope for them through these years of teaching? What are they if any and why?

17. What do you think your students hope for? Do you think there's any change since their entrance? What are they if any and why?

18. Could you name one or two of your most favorite students? In what ways do they excel other students?

19. Would you tell me something about a couple of your successful graduated students? What do you think make them successful?

20. Who is the most creative student in your class? Why do you think he/she is creative?

21. How is the creative student in other respects, e.g. study and cooperation? What hope do you have for him/her?

22. What do you think is the role of creativity in the course of teaching English?

23. What do you think is the role of creativity in students' English study?

24. Do you agree with the declaration that English majors are comparatively less creative than undergraduates of other majors? Why?

Note that although many questions listed above are plural, they would have to be asked separately in actual interviews. Naturally, since these questions were used in semi-structured interviews, many of them were changed considerably in accordance with the real situations.

Appendix II   Interview Transcript Sample

I .Chinese version for Interview with Yu Laoshi（EET1）（Excerpt）
INTERVIEWER：任教10年来，你对教学产生过什么样的困惑呢？
YU LAOSHI：你指的是哪方面的困惑，是对自己而言还是对学生而言？
INTERVIEWER：如果您不介意的话，请先从自己谈起好了。
YU LAOSHI：在初期的困难主要还是对自己的困惑，刚调来的时候也就大学毕业，也没有什么进修提高，虽然读过所谓的研究生主要课程进修班，但是总感觉到水平还是不够。总是在想要通过什么办法将自己的知识水平提到一定的高度，以应付教学，虽说教学效果总的来说不算差，但是花费的精力是非常非常大的，那个时候，为了备好一节课，得要找很多的资料，想很多的办法。那么，读了这个班以后，从理论方面等都有了更广阔的背景知识，所以读了这几年以后，一方面通过教学经验的积累，得到理论知识方面的扩充，更重要的是通过学习，它提供了一个在你自己喜欢的领域里给你一个更为广阔的空间，这几年从学术上对我的帮助是非常大的，虽说上的课时比较有限，但自己在下面读的东西很多、很广。就是随便捧起一个方面的领域都可以深入得下去，在这一点上收获是非常大的。这里读完了以后，我又去了澳大利亚一年，去年才回来。通过这么几年的锻炼，应该说是在理论上的锻炼，还有在国外直接跟 native speaker 之间的接触和生活交往，现在的感觉就好多了。对于学生的困惑呢，主要就是说，应该说以前这种感觉是不明显，我教你学嘛，这是天经地义的，但是这几年的学生，刚回来以后，怎么样呢，老拿他们和我们的过去相比，觉得他们在很多方面不如我的过去。我说的主要是在学习的主动性方面。主动性方面他们远远不如我们过去。在对知识的这种渴望也好，他们的雄心壮志也好，是不如我们以前，可能是代沟的缘故吧，相差很大，再一个方面，可能他们一直都很顺，小学、中学、大学，没有经历过什么艰难困苦，所以感觉到就是学习上很皮。一个班教下来，你就感觉到出类拔萃的学生不多，基本上都是属于那种勉强跟着走，当然学校课时安排等方面也有原因，但是他们自己的刻苦的那种精神是远远不够的，所以我觉得学生的困惑就是说一方面缺乏 motivation，一种进取的精神，另一方面就是尽管现在条件很好了,有各种外在条件都能保证他们学好英语,但是能够真正把它们用在学习上的不多,也应该庆幸的是在现在的社会快速发展的过程中,他们也会相应地受到影响,思维会比较活跃,但问题是应该怎么把他们这种活跃的思维引导到我认为应该的就是学习意义上的层次或者方向上,现在还是一个很大的困惑,感觉到很难、很难。所以我的感觉是我在这方面已经做了很多很多,但是在做了那么多努力后,现在还是收效甚微吧!

INTERVIEWER:您能具体一点,谈谈在促进学生的创造力方面,你采取了哪些方法或措施吗?

YU LAOSHI:首先在二年级到三年级应该是一个相互脱离的过程,应该是一个从初级向高级转化的过程,很多同学一开始都难适应,没有这种思想准备。他的学习方式总的来说还是停留在一个老师说了算,老师叫你做什么你就做什么,教他一课,他绝对不会去学两课,就是这样一种非常被动,非常听话的学习方式,因为你毕竟已经到了一种高层次的学习嘛,基础英语不再应该占很大的比例了,为什么呢,因为从初中开始中学的六年加上大学的两年,八年的学习,基础的学习应该是足够了。现在的问题是怎样在原来的基础上将他们拔高一步,进入三年级以后,也许是教研组内部的关系没有协调好,那么你对他们这种很高的期望,最后会以失望而告终,因为他们在很多方面都还是以一种非常被动的方面来进行的,老师说什么就是什么,没有自己的思想,所以我现在是能够尽可能地鼓励他们有点自己的思想和看法,自己的方式。所以现在因为课时很有限,每周三节,老师就只能够是结合课文的内容,然后在课文内容之外,扩大一些他们的视野,(或者)教他们一些学习的方法,所以三年级上学期主要就是给他们一些跟课文相关的内容去读,读了以后呢,扩大他们的知识量。比方说涉及宗教问题,文化差异问题,中西方文化,包括非洲文化受西方文化的影响等等内容在上课的时候给他们融和进去,在讲课文的时候给他讲,所以有时一篇课文有时上得很长,其实主要不是在讲现象啊或者课文上的内容,而是在讲课外的内容,再比如说环境问题,那是在课文当中透露出来的信息,而不是直截了当的内容,但是我们转一个角度来看这个问题,我们就涉及英国政府对环境保护的态度,当年殖民者移民到美洲大陆以后对环境做了一些人为的破坏,当时为了求生存,当时的状况以及后来对环境所做的很多破坏,这也是可以理解的。但是一旦你扎下根来以后,你应该做些什么东西,然后将美国的现状与中国的现状进行比较,尽最大的努力吧,从这些方面去引导学生,到了下一步,就是到了下一个学期,要求他们读的东西就要难一点了,比如说 Gorge Well, Gage Lorrence 一些比较大的作家他们所写的东西,我们课文中选了他们的一些东西,但这些东西比较狭窄,比较狭隘。学生不能很深刻地理解这些人的风格也好或者背景,从这些方面又加大

Section A　TEFL and Beyond TEFL:Indicators of Creativity Among Chinese EFL Majors and Their Teachers

很多的阅读量吧！每一篇课文,都要记一篇其他的文章,让他们去读,读了以后让他们来问。课堂上没有时间讲,但是要做笔头上的检查,检查的就是他们通过读这些东西以后去发挥他们的思维和想象力,然后让他们去评论哪一句、哪一段给他的感觉最深。这也是开始的阶段,就是从写的方面来练,这样,我觉得还是收到了一定的效果,这样毕竟是给了学生一种自由想象的空间,不再是我老师说这个现象是这样,他就跟着你说这样,这样反过来,等回到课文上,他们对课文上的内容的理解也就要深刻得多,就能够涉及一个比较广阔的空间,不再是课文上说的是什么意思就是什么意思,所以在激发他们的思想能力和想象力方面就有一定的好处,到最后一步,更难一点的阶段,可能就直接给他们一篇原作了。我给过他们一篇 Lorrence 的很长的一篇,也不是很长,像中篇这样的,那么程度也还是比较难的,叫他们下去读,然后让他们以论文的形式,给他们几个选择吧,让他们下去写,写感想也好,评论也好,因为这不是什么严格意义上的批评文章,毕竟我们还没有涉及那么专业化的评论,但是要给他们以充分的想象空间,这个过程比较长,大概一个多月,从我跟他们交流的情况来看,他们的思维能力就有了很大的进步,我发现他们注意到的看到的就不再是语言本身了,就能看到更远的东西,比如说,其中的一个小男孩老是处在阴影里面,然后穿他父亲改过的衣服,从这一点上,学生就能联想到很多很多,比如说,当时的社会背景啊,然后劳伦斯为什么老是把他处理了放在阴影的前景里,光线不是很强的地方,是有一种什么样的用心,可能会是什么什么,有时他们的这种想象会有失偏颇吧,但这总是开始的第一步吧,还有一个困惑呢,就是我们现在的教材很大限度上还是在强调一个基础,后面还是练习啊,词汇练习啊,等等,那么如何把这些内容与发展培养学生的思维能力结合起来,这还在摸索阶段。已经摸索了几年了,因此我几年来一直在做这种探索,一直在想办法,我不希望学生只懂得课本上的那点东西,我希望他们能有一种很活跃的思维能力和想象力,充分地表达自己的思想,哪怕你的思想是比较偏激,甚至是错误的,只要你能够以理服人,因为时间很少,四节课的时间很难让你能有一个别的很完整的交流,只能通过课外的时间、课余时间和通过他们的作业来看。所以,整个教学都处在一种非常困难的过程之中,但一直都在努力。如果仅仅就是课本上的那点内容来说现有的课时是足够了,但是问题是我要给他们搞很多课外的东西,关键是这些东西又比较花费时间……

　　INTERVIEWER:学生的答案与标准答案差别比较大的时候你又是怎么处理的呢？

　　YU LAOSHI:只要表达是准确的,绝对是算他对,而且是鼓励他跟答案上不一样,这只是一部分,其实我们还给他很多课本以外的其他作业,中翻英也好,英翻中也好,从他们的反馈来看,他们很喜欢这样的作业,他们更喜欢额外给他的作业,而不喜欢课本上的作业。但这也没办法,因为考试的时候涉及这课本上方面的内容,所以必须过,但投入的时间和精力相对要少一点,拉得很快。

INTERVIEWER：你所希望的理想的学生是什么样的?

YU LAOSHI：老师都有同样一个愿望,就是希望自己的学生出类拔萃,超过自己,然后语言表达尽可能完美,知识面尽可能的广,思想尽可能的丰富,我希望我的学生就是这样的,我不希望自己的学生呆呆板板,老师告诉你什么,你就相信什么。我实际上对学生挺凶的,经常骂他们,不是骂,是批评他们。有的时候说的话还很重,希望他们摆脱那种惰性,希望他们有自己的思想,而不是 copy 或看 follow 别人的,自己应该有自己的看法……

Ⅱ.INTERVIEWER：What puzzles have you come across in the past 10 years of teaching in×××？

YU LAOSHI：What aspect of puzzles do you mean, puzzles in myself or puzzles in my students？

INTERVIEWER：Please start from yourself, if you don't mind.

YU LAOSHI：In the very beginning when I just graduated from college, the puzzles existed in myself. Without much further study, I always felt my level insufficient although I had studied in a so-called "Training class of main postgraduate courses". I was always seeking for means to enhance my knowledge and ability up to a good level so that I could deal with teaching work well. Although the teaching turned out to be good as a whole, I certainly spent a tremendous amount of energy. At that time, in order to teach for one hour, I had to find a lot of materials and rack my brain for different ideas. Then I attended the××× MA program, and learnt a lot of theoretical background knowledge. Therefore, after these years of accumulation of teaching experiences and broadening of theoretical knowledge, especially through the MA program, I have been provided a much wider space in the field that I like so much. I have been benefited a great deal academically in the past few years. Although we didn't spend a lot of time listening to lectures, we read really extensively after class time. Just pick up a domain of knowledge and we would feel it easy to probe it into depth. After the MA program was finished, I went to study in Australia for one year and got back just last year. After these years of training, especially theoretical study, plus the direct routine contact with native speakers, I feel much better now. Puzzles about students mainly exist in…I must say, it was not obvious before, I teach and you learn, it's God's truth. But the students in the recent years, when I just got back, how about them, I always try to compare them with our past, and always feel that they are far worse than us in those old days. Their lust for knowledge and their ambition are all not as good as our past. Maybe this is a generation gap, very different. Another aspect maybe that they have been always leading very smooth life, they have rarely experienced any rough situations. Therefore, I always feel that they are really sluggish in their study.

You cannot find many outstanding students in a class that you teach, most of them are just following after a fashion. Of course, the school is also to blame regarding curriculum arrangement. However, their hard-working spirit is far from enough. Therefore, my puzzle in students is, on one hand, they are short of motivation and go-aheadism. On the other hand, although their various external conditions are very good to ensure that they can learn English well, but they make good use of very few of these. They are lucky to be born in such a fast-developing society where they would be influenced in certain ways and their thinking would be fostered in full swing. The issue is how such active thinking could be directed toward what I believe to be right, that is toward learning or this direction. This is still an immense puzzle and I feel it very, very difficult. Therefore, my feeling is that I have done a lot without much harvest, very little harvest.

INTERVIEWER: Would you please be a little more concrete as to what you have done? What measures have you taken to foster their creativity?

YU LAOSHI: First of all, grade three (study) is a different process separate from grade two. It is a process that step upward from primary level to advanced level. Many students find it difficult to adapt to this process; they don't have any preparation for it. Their learning style still stays that teacher have all the say—you just do whatever your teachers ask you to do. If the teacher has taught them one lesson, they would never learn two—very passive and obedient. They don't have their independent thinking. Since they are at an advanced level, basic English should no more take up a large proportion. Why?

Having learnt English for 6 years at middle school plus 2 years of college study, altogether 8 years of English learning, their basic learning should be sufficient for a more advanced level. Fundamental English learning should no more take up a large part of their learning time. The issue now is how should we raise their level one step higher from their beginning level. As soon as they entered grade three, maybe it's because that the internal relationship in the Teaching and Research Group have not been well negotiated, your high expectation for the students will only end with despair, because they learn very passively in many aspects. Whatever teachers tell them is seen to be truth. They don't have their own mind. So I always try to encourage them to have their own ideas and opinions as well as their own styles. So, now, since the class time is very limited, only three hours per week. I can only incorporate the content of the text, then broaden their views beyond the texts themselves, or teach them some learning methods. In the first semester of the third year, I would ask the students to read something related to the content of texts they are learning so that their relevant knowledge is increased. For example, articles relating to religious issues, cultural differences, Sino-Western cultural issues, including how African culture is influenced by the Western culture, I would infuse these into my teaching, and, I would give them such relevant articles to read after class. Sometimes, one lesson would take a long time to complete. In fact, most of the time is not spent to teach the superficial meaning of the text itself, but on the content beyond the text. For example, I used to teach them a lesson related to environment, just related, it's not strictly about environment. I changed the angle of seeing it and we involved the attitude of the British Government toward environmental protection. When the colonists first moved to the American Continent, they did some damage to the environment. At that time, they did all these in order to survive, thus all these damage that they had done to the environment was understandable. However, as soon as they settled down, what did they have to do? After that, the event was compared with the current American and Chinese situations. I just try such things with my efforts, to lead the students to think. The next step is the second semester. I would ask them to read something rather difficult, for example, works written by some great authors like Gorge Well and Gage Lorrence. There are some excerpts in their textbook, but they are rather narrow and limited. The students cannot deeply understand the writing styles or background of these authors. They are requested to increase a lot of reading in this respect. Some other articles should accompany every text. They are required to read these articles and then ask questions about them. We don't have time to explain these articles. But their written work about these articles should be checked. I ask them to write about their remarks about the paragraphs, or sentences that have most impressed them. This helps them to develop their thinking and imagination and I think it has turned out to be rather effective. They do not have to follow their teacher's thinking. They are given a space for free imagination. When they return to the text, instead of being limited to what the text tells them, they would generally find their understanding a lot deeper and they are able to involve a much wider space in thinking. Therefore, it can do good to their thinking and imaginative ability. Then, after this stage, I would give them a complete piece of rather difficult original writing to read and ask them to write an essay about it. I would give them several choices. They could choose to write a commentary or critical journal about it. It does not have to be critical essay in any strict sense, since the students have never learned anything as professional as that. But they should be provided with bountiful room for free imagination. This process is rather long, about one month or so. From my observation about my current students, I have observed a major progress in their thinking ability. What they can see is no more mere surface of the language, but something deeper inside. For instance, in the novel, there is a boy, who always stands in the shadows, wearing clothes adjusted from his father's. Just from this point, the students can think about a lot. For example, the social background at that time, and the reasons that Lorrence always locates him in shadowy backgrounds. What could be the author's intention? His purpose could be this or that. Sometimes, such imagination of theirs could be lopsided, but it's the beginning step. Another puzzle is that our textbook, in a great extent, still put emphasis on basics. There are still exercises, vocabulary exercises, etc. How can these be merged in cultivating students' thinking ability is still to be groped for. Several years already, and I'm still after such groping, still thinking about means to solve it. I don't hope to see that my students can only understand what the textbook tells them. I hope to see in them very active thinking and imagination, see that they can fully express their ideas. Even if their ideas may be rather radical, or even wrong, their argument should be complimented as far as they can make it acceptable to others. Four hours of teaching hardly gives you opportunity to fulfill a complete communication. I could only use spare time or after class time and see (their ideas) through exercises. So, the whole teaching is undergoing a very difficult process, but I've been always trying hard to do it well. Time would be good enough if only the bit of content in the textbook had to be dealt with. Problem is that I would like to do lots of things after the class time, especially because these things are all very time-consuming…

INTERVIEWER: What do you do when the students' answers are different from the standard key to the exercises?

YU LAOSHI: As far as their expressions are correct, I would count them right. Actually I encourage them to be different from the key. This is only one part (of exercises). In fact, we would give them other exercises beyond the textbook to do: Chinese-English or English-Chinese translation. According to their feedback, they like such exercises very much. They like these extra exercises more than those from the textbook. However, I can't do much because the exercises from the textbooks are to be included in the tests. We have to go through them but with much less time and energy. We had to go through these very quickly.

INTERVIEWER: What kind of students are the most ideal, according to your opinion?

YU LAOSHI: All the teachers have a common wish, that is to say, they hope their students to be superb and can surpass the teachers themselves. My students may surpass me. They ought to be perfect in their English expression, wide in content knowledge and rich in their thinking. I don't hope my students are rigid and take trust in whatever their teachers tell them. In fact, I'm rather strict with my students. I often scold them, well, not scold them, but criticize them. Sometimes, my words were really very serious. I do hope that can get rid of their laziness I hope that they have their own thinking, not just copy or follow others' ideas. They should have their own independent thinking…

SECTION B

Theories and Practice:
Exploring Creative TEFL Methodology
in the Chinese Context

理论与实践：
探索在中国环境下的创造性
英语教学之路

CHAPTER 1
CULTIVATING PLURALISTIC THINKING THROUGH LITERATURE TEACHING
——Teaching *Jane Eyre* and *Wide Sargasso Sea* as an example

1.1 Introduction

When "quality education" is drawing wide attention of the present Chinese educational field, some scholars are especially concerned about the overall low ability of many undergraduate English majors, which results in the shortage of outstanding people among the students in the academic field or in their practical work after graduation. Liu Yi (2000) imputes it to the excessive concentration on the students' language skill training itself while having largely neglected their thinking ability training. They are too much used to all the imitation exercises in the language training and accepting the standard answers sourced from their teachers. Therefore, they are generally not excellent in offering their pluralistic or creative ideas, an obvious display of their low problem-solving ability. The literature of English is a most ideal course for the students to train and pluralize their thinking if properly tapped. However, the literature teacher of English cannot simply plunge them into the ocean of discussion from the beginning. He/she will find the students not doing much talking, because they have been kept in the jail of standard answers and authoritative opinions for too long, and they are not confident enough to voice their own ideas. It is therefore the teacher's basic responsibility to break the psychological locks and bars for the students so that they are courageous enough to challenge the authorities and pluralize their literary understanding. This paper argues that the students' pluralistic thinking habit can be effectively cultivated in the literature teaching of English, as will be illustrated in the teaching of Charlotte Bronte's *Jane Eyre* integrated with Jean Rhys' *Wide Sargasso Sea*.

1.2 Students' Normal Response to "*Jane Eyre*"

Jane Eyre is such a well-know novel among the Chinese students that most of them may have either read its Chinese version or watched the translated film of the story by the time they formally study it in the English literature course. However, when the students are asked to respond to the story, they are most likely to give very similar answers, or even a strictly universal answer. For them, Bronte's *Jane Eyre* is impressive chiefly for two reasons. First of all, the students are deeply moved by the "pure love" between the plain-looking, but intelligent and self-confident heroine and the rich squire of Thornfield, Mr. Rochester; they are also happy to see the ultimate realization of their seemingly disinterested marriage at the end of the story with the death of Bertha, Mr. Rochester's mad wife, in a fire and the final removal of their barrier. Secondly, having been taught Marxism, the students are also keen to see the class struggle between proletarians represented by *Jane Eyre* and bourgeoisie as represented by Mrs. Reed and her children as well as Mr. Brocklehurst, the school manager. Attracted by Jane's frankness and her great courage in fighting against the oppressing class, the students never get the feeling that Jane, as the narrator of the story, would ever try to varnish the truth. Also, the narrator has quite successfully presented her foes and friends before the readers. As a result, the students usually fall into the world of Jane and would tend to watch everything through her eyes, which is obviously intended by the author for all her readers. They would, for example, dislike Mrs. Reed or Blanche Ingram merely because Jane did; they would also dislike Bertha, the mad woman in the attic, as the barrier of an ideal marriage between Jane and Mr. Rochester to be removed.

Seeing all such pre-knowledge and interpretations of the students about the literary work, many literature teachers may tend to consider it a good chance to skip the novel at that without bothering with any more follow-ups. Keeping in mind the urgent need of cultivating the students' critical or pluralistic spirit, however, a more responsible teacher would be quick to see the vantage of better utilizing their familiarity with this novel and inspire their individual thinking from some different angles. The teacher can further expand their view by introducing feminist theory first in combination with *Wide Sargasso Sea* and ignite their independent pluralistic thinking from there.

1.3　Introducing Feminism Through "Wide Sargasso Sea"

> Feminist criticism, which ranges from the scholarly to the political and prescriptive, seeks to re-examine women's literature of the past and present with the aid of a new feminist awareness ("raised consciousness") of female and male stereotypes, women's economic situation as authors, the supposed prejudice of male critics and publishers, the relationship between writing and gender, etc. (Oxford Companion to English Literature. 1993:344)

Feminism in a broader sense is not just concerned about female bias, it also comments on prejudice or oppression relating to race, class, religion, nationality, culture and age, etc. Analyzing *Jane Eyre* through feminist view will be quite a new experience for the Chinese students and will serve as an exciting start for mind-opening warm-up exercise.

However, instead of laying hands directly on the theoretical explanation, the students' attention can be directed to Bertha, the mad woman locked up in the attic. They should be encouraged to take a critical new look at the insane Mrs. Rochester in *Jane Eyre*, think about her former beauty and rich dowry, consider Rochester's wealth and his reasons for marrying her, then imagine how Bertha could become mad and be imprisoned in the attic. The students can then discuss about various possibilities behind the scene and try to fill up the part of story about Bertha for Bronte. Before they do it, however, they should be warned to drop any possible stereotypes and make Bertha as the narrator if possible. It might sound a queer request for the students because of their former unfavorable mindset about her. Now that the students' stories are made up and reported, Jean Rhys' *Wide Sargasso Sea* may be introduced to them and they can then compare it with the stories they made on their own.

In believing that Bertha has not been fairly treated in *Jane Eyre* since she was depicted as a horrible nightmare and a greatly marginalized hideous barrier of a desired marriage, Jean Rhys chose to make a heroine of the white Creole lady in her *Wide Sargasso Sea* and described her as a passionate nature-loving beauty, a victim of the loveless marriage with the hypocritical, merciless and revenge- filled Mr. Rochester who had been attracted by her beauty and fortune. The students' attention may be drawn to the last section of the novel (P.174), where Rhys encourages the reader to believe in Antoinette's (Bertha's) recovery while portraying her in actions that we know are "insane" from *Jane Eyre*. They would experience a gradual emotional and attitudinal conflict or change about Antoinette when they know that she had regained her sanity but was still locked up in a small room where there was only "one window high up-you cannot see out of it" (P.179), where "there is no looking-glass" and she did not know what she was like (P.180), from where she hoped that Richard would take her away "because it is so cold and dark" (P.183), and where she could have been given much better food because "they're rich enough" (P.186). Now comes the chance to further challenge the students with the question, "why did Antoinette become mad in the first place?" By being lead back to the second part of the novel (P.65), where Rochester had a much more detailed description of their marriage, the students would know that he had planned to marry the heiress mainly in order to obtain the 30,000-pound dowry from her. After the marriage, he found that Antoinette did not fit for his English taste at all, and he began to define and reinforce his values upon her. He renamed her as "Bertha"; he labeled her to be sexually promiscuous and hence mentally unbalanced; and eventually he reduced her from a vibrant woman in a vibrant land to be a ghost-like woman in an attic. As Abel (1979: P.157) put it, "…the definition and reinforcement of values by men can drive women to deny their own experience, an act that lays the ground work for a schizoid mental state."

The new views that the students have developed from *Wide Sargasso Sea* will enable them to recall what they previous learn from *Jane Eyre* with much more critical ideas about Rochester and Bertha. Important is the above teaching procedure in the fact that the students are then given enough courage to challenge their former understanding, even the authority of the writer or critics.

1.4 Reviewing "*Jane Eyre*" from a Feminist's Point of View

As soon as their attention was directed to the description of the red-room in which Jane was locked up by Mrs. Reed as a punishment (P.13), the students will be able to feel about the similar helplessness and desperation resided in both of the women when confined and cut up from the outside. Both of them needed to escape imprisonment: little Jane escaped from the ghastly atmosphere of the red room by losing her consciousness, while Bertha tried to kill herself and destroy her other "self" (Antoinette) in order to win complete "freedom". Another similarity between the two women may also include their dependence on love and marriage as the only means of self-realization: she who loses it loses the entire world and she who wins it wins the eternal happiness. Further more, both women were oppressed and subjugated to the patriarchal society in one way or another: Bertha was an absolute victim of Rochester's man chauvinism and Jane, who appeared to be the winner of the game, also fell into the traditional role of a whole-hearted housewife in the end. Now is a good point for the teacher to escort the students into the discussion of the women's situation in China and in the Western countries today as well as in the past.

Since it is obvious for the students to see the differences between Bertha and Jane as are depicted in *Jane Eyre*, it might be more meaningful for the teacher to deepen their thinking with questions such as: Why did Bronte decide to portray Antoinette as an abominable mad woman who turned out to be Rochester's wife and a barrier of an ideal marriage? How do you judge the importance of the mad woman's existence in the structure of the novel? During the discussion, however, the teacher may ask them to keep in mind the nationalities of the characters and the author as a pre-feminist, thus their thinking will be illuminated and they will be ready to discuss about racial discrimination, colonialism, and the author's unconscious warning to other rebellious women.

1.5 Beyond Feminist Criticism

However, the introduction of feminist criticism is not the end of the teacher's work. The students' view still needs to be further broadened from other angles of criticism and make sure that the students do not regard what they have agreed upon in their former discussion as the only standard answers.

For instance, the teacher may ask the students to consider how different narrative voices can influence the specific ways in which the same story is told (Jordan, 1993). The class may also be requested to critically review all the descriptions about fire and light in *Jane Eyre* (Burgan, 1993), and then compare them against those in *Wide Sargasso Sea*. They may as well discuss about the centrality of colonial sources for identity, both economic and psychological through Jane's inheritance, Rochester's first marriage and fortune, and St. John's spiritual mission (Kucich, 1993). It's never too much for them even to discuss about the construction of the novel itself through the most radical criticism about Bronte and her works such as, "She had no gift of form, no restraint, little power of observation, no power of analysis. And her novels suffer from it. They are badly constructed, they are improbable, they are often ridiculous (Cecil, 1931)." In a word, the students are free to explore the novel with whatever elements and from whichever angles they feel the most challenging, interesting and thought provoking.

In summary, Chinese undergraduates of English major are traditionally educated to adore authorities and accept their ideas completely and passively. This tendency has strongly hindered their ability development, and their lack of pluralistic thinking does not suit for the heated competition in the modern world. Through the teaching of *Jane Eyre* in combination with *Wide Sargasso Sea*, this paper has demonstrated the important role of a literature teacher of English in "quality education", and he/ she is encouraged to always keep an eye on opportunities available for cultivating the students' pluralistic thinking. Along with the pluralistic thinking cultivation in the literature teaching, in time, the teacher will be more than happy to find that the students are greatly improved in their English communicative competence and their motivation in learning literature of English is much increased.

References:

Abel, Elizabeth. Women and Schizophrenia: The Fiction of Jean Rhys. Contemporary Literature, 1979, 20 (2): 157. Board of Regents of the University of Wisconsin System.

Bronte, Charlotte. *Jane Eyre*. Oxford University Press & Foreign Language Teaching and Research Press, 1847.

Burgan, Mary. Fire and Light in *Jane Eyre*. In Hoeveler D. & Lau B. (Ed.) Approaches to Teaching Bronte's *Jane Eyre*, 1993: 82-86. New York: The Modern Language Association of America.

Cecil, D.. Charlotte Bronte. In his Early Victorian Novelists: Essays in Revaluation, 1935: 119-54. The Bobbs-Merriall Company.

Jean Rhys. *Wide Sargasso Sea*. Norton Paperback by arrangement with the Wallace Literary Agency, Inc, 1966.

Jordan, J. O.. Teaching specific Contexts: *Jane Eyre* and Narrative Voice. In Hoeveler D. & Lau B. (Ed.) Approaches to Teaching Bronte's *Jane Eyre*, 1993: 76-81. New York: The Modern Language Association of America.

Kucich, John. *Jane Eyre* and Imperialism. In Hoeveler D. & Lau B. (Ed.) Approaches to Teaching Bronte's *Jane Eyre*, 1993: 104-109. New York: The Modern Language Association of America.

Liu, Yi. Course Construction for Foreign Language Majors of Higher Education. Foreign Language World, 2000(3): 12

Oxford University Press & Foreign Language Teaching and Research Press. Feminist criticism. In Oxford Companion To English Literature, 1993: 344.

CHAPTER 2
MAXIMIZING THE EXPERTISE OF NATIVE ENGLISH SPEAKING TEACHERS IN CHINA

2.1 Introduction

Every year, thousands of native English speaking teachers (called foreign teachers hereafter) are employed to teach English in various colleges and universities in China. They are becoming an increasingly important component of TEFL in Chinese higher education. However, reports indicate that there are frequently problems between foreign teachers and Chinese students arising from Chinese students' expectations and foreign teachers' performance (Li, 1999: 144). Recruitment of non-qualified personnel, lack of clearly defined teaching objectives for the teachers (Maley, 1983), and improper utilization of their teaching skills are some of the reported reasons for these problems. The resulting negative reports about foreign teachers have, to some extent, affected the great enthusiasm of many school administrators in further expanding their foreign staff.

Have our foreign colleagues really betrayed our trust? The current paper found, by comparing the teaching features and roles of foreign teachers and those of their Chinese colleagues (called Chinese teachers hereafter), that the present situation is much more optimistic than has so far been interpreted by many people. Their unique advantages can be utilized as important supplemental elements in the current Chinese TEFL system when properly tapped on. Instead of blaming the foreign teachers for not having fulfilled the high and often misled expectations, we really need to re-examine the positive values of employing foreign teachers, then decide what can be done to maximize their expertise.

2.2 The Study: Process and Results

For the study, 21 second-year and 25 third-year English majors from a university in Kunming as well as 21 first-year English majors from another college to the Northwest of Kunming were chosen as the survey subjects. Each of these students was asked to generalize their opinions about their foreign teachers and Chinese teachers by making choices among items listed. The survey was written in Chinese.

The first question for the students is, "By comparing foreign teachers and Chinese Teachers, which of the following characteristics do you think to be more typical of Chinese teachers and which ones more typical of Chinese teachers?" (Refer to Chart 1 for results).

The second question in the questionnaire is, "Which subjects do you think are more suitable for foreign teachers and which ones more proper for Chinese teachers?" (Please refer to Chart 2 for results)

For group interviews, two groups of English majors, each consisting of 4 students, were randomly chosen from both second-year and third-year classes in the university. The students were interviewed in two separate groups and the discussion was carried out in Chinese mandarin in a very casual atmosphere. I took notes of views expressed and no tape-recording was implemented. By doing so, I believe that the students would feel completely free to express their ideas. Apart from the group interviews, I also talked with a number of students and teachers (Chinese as well as foreign teachers). In such occasions, notes were only taken after the dialogue when something noticeable was brought up during the talk.

中国环境下的创造性英语教学探索
Searching for Creativity in the Chinese TEFL Context

Chart 1 Foreign Teachers & Chinese Teachers Viewed by Students

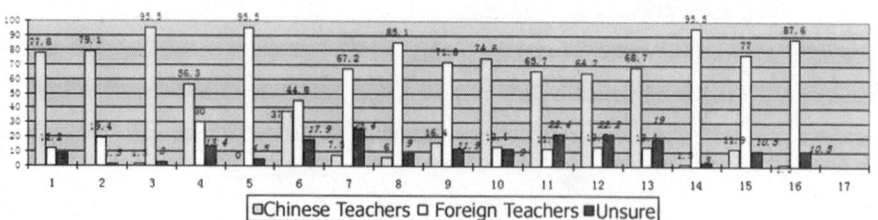

Note:

1 = *They are stricter with students*

2 = *They know better about ourreal English level*

3 = *They organize teaching more lively and more interestingly*

4 = *We can understand their English better*

5 = *We are more willing to speak English with them outside the classroom*

6 = *They teach us more patiently and more carefully*

7 = *They respect us more and are more friendly*

8 = *They give us more opportunities to speak English in class*

9 = *Dealing with them make us feel more about the importance of studying English*

10 = *They understand our difficulties in learning English better*

11 = *They can enable us to understand and master what we learn more effectively*

12 = *They prepare their lessons more carefully and abundantly*

13 = *Their teaching is organized more in line with our real level*

14 = *We can learn about English-speaking countries' cultural background knowledge from them*

15 = *We are more motivated to learn English from them*

16 = *Their teaching provokes more of our creative thinking*

Chart 2 Trust for Curriculum Teaching

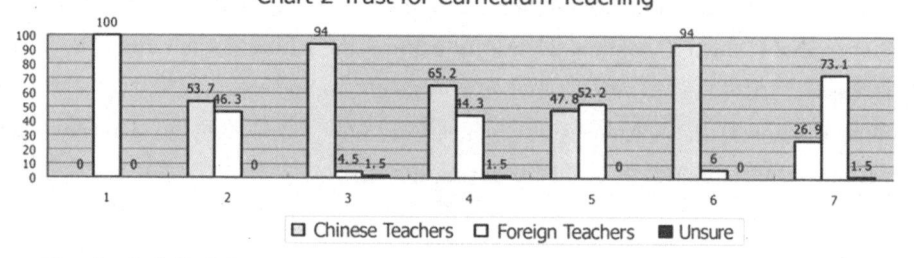

Note: 1 = *Oral English*

2 = *Listening*

3 = *Intensive Reading*

4 = *Extensive Reading*

5 = *Writing*

6 = *Grammar*

7 = *Pronunciation*

8 = *Literature*

2.3 Discussions

2.3.1 Teacher-student relationship

As the figures in Chart 1 show, 67.2% of the students believe that their foreign teachers are more friendly and pay more respect to their students, compared with only 7.5% who felt just the opposite (25.3% were unsure). This result tends to confirm established research relating to differences between the Asian culture and the Western culture. A teacher in Asia is an authority figure in relationship to his or her students and the teacher owes his or her authority to the students and the students owe their respect to the teacher (Scollon & Wong-Scollon, 1991). Owing to this academic "superiority" of the teachers to their students, the students generally obey their teachers without regard to right or wrong, and any intimate teacher-student friendship would be regarded as "improper". However, in Western countries, everyone is seen to be more or less equal, no matter whether he/she is a teacher or a student, old or young. In Australian universities, students may call some lecturers by their first names, and are encouraged to challenge, question and argue with their instructors (Ginsburg, 1992). A Canadian teacher even asked his blind Chinese students to touch his nose with their hands in his first English class in order to gain familiarity and friendship (Wu, 1999). In an American school (Wang, 2000), the principal and the teachers were often seen to stand at the main gate and welcome their students attending the school in the morning. In the school, students' scores on tests would be always kept confidential, only being accessible to the relevant individuals and no one in the class is neglected or belittled.

The casual and friendly relationship between foreign teachers and Chinese students as indicated in the current study might be seen to be a natural transference of Western culture into the Chinese context and is widely appreciated by their students.

2.3.2 Motivation and interest

As many as 95.5% of the students agree that foreign teachers organize teaching in a more lively and more interesting way. Li Beilan (1999) observed that Australian primary schools are filled with leisurely atmosphere, and the teachers teach while "playing" with the kids. Yang Zhenning also noticed (Zhou, 2000) that American children would quickly grow impatient with what they are doing and give it up as soon as it fails to attract them. This characteristic is very unlike the Chinese children, who are used to step-by-step learning. Foreign teachers, who themselves have been brought up in such a society, would naturally value highly of the students' motivation and interest in what they are supposed to learn. Many students admitted that they had been greatly impressed by the ability of their foreign teachers in organizing vivid classroom activities that invited the participation of all of their students. Experienced foreign teachers are always ready to adjust their teaching to maintain the student's interest and to keep their motivation at a high level (Refer to Smith, 1996 concerning the description of a vivid classroom argument).

"Interest is the best teacher." Krashen's affective filter hypothesis also suggests that high motivation will lower students' affective filter and thus increase the intake for language acquisition (Krashen & Terrell, 1983). This study shows that most of our foreign teachers are doing a superb job in this respect.

2.3.3 Acquired language competence and learned linguistic knowledge

It is not surprising to find that as many as 94% of the students would prefer Chinese teachers rather than foreign teachers to teach intensive reading and English grammar courses (refer to Chart 2). It has been commonly accepted in China that one cannot learn a foreign language without learning its linguistic rules. Chinese teachers of English themselves exclusively learned the language through very detailed study of grammar, vocabulary and phonetics in a bottom-up process. In other words, they have gained the language proficiency chiefly through learning process. Krashen (1983:26) defined learning as "explicit" knowledge of rules, being aware of them and being able to talk about them. However, most foreign teachers, who acquired the language in L1 environment, would not generally be "aware" of the rules of the language they have acquired (unless he/she has majored in or somehow studied it intentionally). Instead, they have a "feel" for correctness: when they hear an error, they may not know exactly what rule was violated, but somehow "know" that an error was committed (ibid:26). Intensive reading and grammar, which require the explicit knowledge of the language for explaining and analyzing the form of the language, place the Chinese teachers in an authoritative position.

Lack of explicit knowledge of the rule system does not affect the unshakeable expertise of a native language speaker in using the language. Obviously, the students are quite aware of this fact, for all of them (100%) unanimously chose foreign teachers to teach them oral English, which is one of the very areas that maximize their expertise in speaking the language and their ability in organizing motivating classroom activities. As noted in Chart 1, 77.6% of the students feel more motivated to learn English from their foreign teachers. Some of them explained that they feel so because they are more confident about the accuracy of their naturally acquired English.

2.3.4 Learning and ability-building

Maley (1983) notes that the traditional Chinese students and teachers view books as an embodiment of knowledge, wisdom and truth. Knowledge is "in" the book and can be taken out and put inside the students' heads. On the contrary, most Westerners regard books only as tools for learning—not the goal of learning. The facts in the books are open to interpretation, the opinions disputed and the ideas discussed. In other words, Chinese students and teachers tend to treat what is in the books as the product of wisdom to be committed to memory, while Western students and teachers regard it as a process towards their real learning. Dr. Yang Zhenning (Zhou, 2000) also observed that traditional Chinese children learn rules and formulas by heart, and then practice using them in various exercises. But American children would be asked to prove the rules and formulas before using them. One approach looks at the product, the other at the process; one looks at accumulating knowledge and the other at cultivating ability.

Liu Yi (2000) shows his concerns over the shortage of outstanding people among the students of English major in the academic field or in their practical work after graduation and he imputes it to over-concentration on the language learning itself while having largely neglected the cultivation of students thinking ability. China has noticed the high-test-scores-but-low-ability phenomenon, which is rather common in many schools, and is taking some measures to correct this tendency. "Quality Education" has been emphasized over and over again by the central government in the recent years, and yet has not flowed over into ideal results, partly due to backwash effects of various competitive tests, and partly due to the fossilization of many teachers' ideology to the traditional teaching.

In this study, 87.6% of the students agreed that their foreign teachers' teaching style provokes more of their creative thinking than their Chinese teachers do. In the interviews, they further explained that many foreign teachers teach with very imaginative and creative methods, and they generally encourage students to contribute their own opinions, especially their critical ideas, which are quite rare in a class taught by Chinese teachers. In this sense, our foreign teachers have helped to fill up much of the gap, and are beneficial in accelerating the reform from the traditional "duck-stuffing" teaching to "Quality Education".

2.3.5　English learning environment

It is a consensus among Chinese teachers, students, and administrators that foreign teachers can help to create an authentic language learning environment which may be difficult even impossible for Chinese teachers to create (Li, 1999:82).

In the study, the majority of the students agree that foreign teachers give them more opportunities to speak English in class (85.1%) and they are more willing to speak English with them outside the classroom (95.5%). When asked about the reasons for the preference, the students made the point that they feel funny or unnatural when they speak in English with their Chinese teachers (especially after class), because it is much easier for them to speak in Chinese for communication purposes. But it becomes necessary to make them understood in English when they are facing a foreign teacher. The communication in English is real and indispensable.

2.3.6　Cultural knowledge for TEFL learners

In many cases, Chinese students fail to understand reading or listening materials in English correctly not just because of their lack in understanding the linguistic form of the language, but also because they are not familiar with the cultural background knowledge of the English speaking countries. On the contrary, all-rounded cultural background knowledge of the countries and the peoples will greatly increase the students' ability in understanding the receptive materials. Meanwhile, students' cross-cultural knowledge will also help to enhance their cultural communicative competence with the native English speakers.

Needless to say, foreign teachers, who are authentic culture-carriers of their native countries, are also the most ideal narrators of their own cultures. As the study shows, 95.5% of the students are sure that they can learn more about the English-speaking countries' cultural background knowledge from their foreign teachers. By face-to-face daily contact with their foreign teachers, the students will not only hear their personal oral explanation about their own cultures, more importantly, they can also observe and sense the shades of differences between the Western and Chinese cultures through what they do and how they respond to the existing culture.

2.4 Minimize Disadvantages and Maximize Advantages

Several things can be done to minimize the disadvantageous perspectives of the foreign English teachers' teaching and maximize their advantages.

2.4.1 Proper allocation of teaching responsibilities

It can be concluded from the previous discussions that foreign teachers have prevailing communicative competence in English. They are much more capable of organizing classroom activities to initiate a language acquisition atmosphere than teaching explicit knowledge about the language, and they are more familiar with a top-down teaching process than bottom-up. Courses like oral English and English writing would be the most ideal to maximize their acquired language competence, while teaching grammar would be most probably a bad choice for them. Listening courses and extensive reading would be a lot more suitable for them than intensive reading. If he/she has received higher education in the English language, teaching courses like literature, which entails the study of language more through a framing of content process while learning the relevant knowledge through the English media, would also help to utilize their teaching competence as well as language ability.

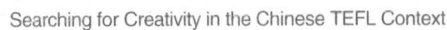

2.4.2 Beyond the classroom

"Many foreign teachers feel cut off and alone" (Maley, 1983). China has changed enormously in the last couple of decades and foreigners are no more treated as a "weird lot". However, many foreign teachers still do not mix with their students very much on a more informal basis. They go to class in class time and are left alone afterwards.

To improve the relationship, the students need to be constantly encouraged to overcome their shyness and get in touch with their foreign teachers. On the other hand, foreign teachers also need to be housed to live more closely with their Chinese colleagues and students, and they should be encouraged to participate in the various activities organized by the students or the school.

Some very successful examples were also observed during the study. In these inspiring examples, the foreign teachers play games with the students, organize English corner for the students, visit students' dorms, invite students to hold parties in their houses, give students extra help with their English pronunciation or listening, and so on. They even join the students for dancing or singing contests. In fact, many students claimed that they had learnt much more from their foreign teachers outside the classroom than inside. It is very true that the English learning atmosphere that active foreign teachers create for students beyond the class can be even more valuable than what they can contribute to the class in a dozen or more periods each week.

2.4.3 Pedagogy and Teacher Training Program

It has been noticed that most foreign teachers use communicative or interactive approaches in their teaching, which is fundamentally different from the traditional Chinese pedagogical doctrines. The communicative approach focuses on speaking activities, involving spontaneous exchanges in unplanned discourse, on fluency, on negotiations of meanings, on problem-solving, skill-building, and on the central role of the learner rather than teacher (Marton, 1988:38-39). The approach applied by most foreign teachers, as was discussed earlier, is successful in motivating their students and in ability-building features.

However, most students (68.7%) in the current study commented that their foreign teachers could not organize their teaching as close to their real level as their

Chinese teachers, and 74.6% of the students made the assumption that their Chinese teachers understand their difficulties in learning English better than their foreign teacher. This must be the biggest problem for most foreign teachers. There are two extremes in this respect. One possibility is that they may be unaware of the fundamental difference in learning process between the first language and that of a foreign language, and neglect the necessity in giving students enough help for comprehension purposes. For example, they may speak too fast or speak with vocabulary beyond the reach of their students; they may ask students to read a difficult passage without giving any explanation about it, etc. Another possibility is that they may become over-conscious about their students' difficulties and try to teach them some very basic grammatical rules without realizing that they learned these rules many years ago. The fact that they cannot produce a sentence correctly does not necessarily mean that they do not consciously know the rules, they just need to be given sufficient opportunities to put them into practice so that the utterances become natural and automatic.

Li (1999:234) argues that foreign teachers need to develop language awareness to enable them to make informed decisions in their teaching and in selecting the teaching methodologies appropriate to the needs and expectations of the students. It is quite true that the language awareness development will enable foreign teachers to locate their teaching more in line with the actual level of the students.

The most direct and simple solution to the problem is obviously to recruit trained and qualified TEFL teachers. This is a rather complicated issue that has not yet been very well coped with so far (Li, 1999:97-104, Maley, 1983). Since it is not easy to recruit fully competent foreign teachers under the existing system, it might be more practical for us to look at the possibilities of either a pre-teaching or an on-going foreign teacher-training program. Such an on-site training program is suggested to basically comprise three integral elements: TEFL Theories and Methodologies, Sino-Foreign-Teacher Mutual Learning, and Chinese.

As many current foreign teachers in China did not major in the English language or TEFL during their higher education, it is necessary for them to learn some theoretical basics and practical methodologies in the field, so that their TEFL awareness is reinforced. Sino-Foreign Teacher Mutual Learning is designed to stimulate communication and dialogues between Chinese teachers and foreign teachers. Rules may need to be set up for foreign teachers to attend Chinese teachers' classes regularly and make comments on their teaching, and the same should be the case with Chinese teachers. Through such attendance, it is hoped that foreign teachers will grow awareness about the real levels of their own students and it may be a perfect chance to reflect upon their own teaching. Chinese teachers too, can benefit from their foreign colleagues' comments or by observing their different teaching strategies. Learning the Chinese language has a dual-purpose. The first is, of course, for their daily necessity of communication. The second purpose is to help them to evolve a better understanding about their students as learners of a foreign language, which is essentially distinct from their native language.

2.4.4 Other responsibilities

In order to exert their expertise, foreign teachers may also need to be involved in other responsibilities of the school they work for. Normally, besides their daily teaching, Chinese teachers in colleges or universities are required to carry out research work like writing textbooks or articles relating to TEFL, and so on. Foreign teachers may be of crucial help to proofread the English books or articles that the Chinese teachers have written. It is a great pity for us to see that our foreign teachers' native competence has not been very well tapped in this area. Hundreds of books or articles have been published with improper expressions that could have been easily spotted by a native expert but may not be observable to a non-native professor. Some foreign teachers complained that they had to spend a lot of time correcting the mistakes in the textbooks they were asked to use in class.

English oral contests or composition competitions can be other activities to include our foreign teachers as judges. They will generally be able to notice something in the language that may be overlooked by us Chinese teachers. With their participation, the results may turn out to be fairer.

To sum up, on the one hand, we should not try to shun from the problem that arises from the teaching of many foreign teachers: the mismatches between the students' real level and the foreign teachers' teaching performance. It is suggested that school administrators should not misplace their teaching roles, and more importantly, an on-site training and exchanging program will be necessary to facilitate the teaching improvement of both foreign teachers and Chinese teachers. On the other hand, it is essential for us to observe the advantageous side of engaging foreign teachers in the Chinese TEFL context and make it possible to maximize their expertise. In order to utilize the expertise of foreign teachers, we need to basically acknowledge their high language proficiency and the effectiveness of their teaching methods. The article has also indicated that foreign teachers may be even more valuable beyond the classroom than inside when properly positioned.

References

Ginsburg, Eliszabeth. Not Just a matter of English. HERDSA News, (1992) 14 /1:6-8

Krashen, S. And T. Terrell The Theoretical Model: Five Hypotheses. The Natural Approach: Language Acquisition in the Classroom. Oxford: Pergamon, 1983.

Li, Bei Lan. Australian Education: Class Time is Kids' Playing Time. Beyond the 8 Hours, 1999(12):30-31

Li, Ming Sheng. Perceptions of the Place of Expatriate English Language Teachers in China. A thesis submitted in total fulfillment of the requirements for the degree of Doctor of Philosophy. Graduate School of Education, Latrobe University, 1999.

Liu, Yi. Course Construction for Foreign Language Majors of Higher Education. Foreign Language World, 2000(3):12.

Maley, Alan. XANADU— "A miracle of rare device": the teaching of English in China. Reprinted, from Language Learning and Communication, 1983 2(1): 97-104

Marton, W.. Methods in English Language Teaching: Frameworks and options. New York: Prentice-Hall, 1988:38-39

Scollon, Ron and Wong-Scollon, Suzanne. Topic confusion in English-Asian discourse. World Englishes, 1991(10/2):113-125

Smith, Kevin J. Cross-cultural Schemata and Change in Modern China: "First Fresh Air Comes in and also Flies Come in". Language and Education, 1996(11/0):1-10

Zhou, Hong Lin. Comparative reflections on Chinese Education and American Education. Educational Reference, 2000(5):46

Wang, Ping. My Views on Teacher-Student Relationship in America. Wide Angle of Information, 2000(11):39

We, Jie. English Teacher of Blind Children Is a Canadian. Beyond the 8 Hours, 2000(10):26-28

CHAPTER 3
RESPONDING TO FAVORS: A CONTRASTIVE STUDY OF GRATITUDE-EXPRESSING STRATEGIES BETWEEN CHINESE AND AMERICANS

3.1 Background

An American friend of mine told me a story about a Chinese teacher of English who once did some translation from Chinese into English and went for his help. It took them about an hour each time for several afternoons discussing about the problems in the English version. He said he felt quite uncomfortable to hear the Chinese teacher say each time when she departed that she was very sorry and embarrassed to have spent so much of his precious time. He said jokingly at last, "If you really feel sorry for the interruption, you shouldn't have come to interrupt me at all." Neither of them realized the fact that she had sociolinguistically transferred what was natural and fully acceptable in her Chinese L1 (first language) into English. However, it was not the only pragmatic misunderstanding I know of. I also heard some foreign students complaining about the impoliteness even ungratefulness about the Chinese students they dealt with who did not express their thanks when they should have. Meanwhile, some of my Chinese colleagues also admitted that most Westerners are very courteous, but they seem to be too polite which can make Chinese feel an insurmountable social distance. Just as one of my Chinese colleagues put it, "They always thank you for however trivial something you have done for them, and they thank you unexceptionally no matter how many years you have been friends with them. " In most cases, neither group realizes the cross-cultural differences in responding to situations where they are benefited by other people's act. They just feel uncomfortable or even upset when they hear something that is unexpected or when they do not hear something that is normally expected in their own culture, and thus experience in cross-cultural miscommunication.

Searle (1969) discusses thanking and sees it as an illocutionary speech act performed by a speaker, and is based on a past act performed by the hearer that benefits the speaker. Meanwhile, the speaker should also believe it to have benefited him/her and feels grateful or appreciative, and thus utters an expression of appreciation. Leech (1983) defines thanking as expressive, since it makes known the speaker's psychological attitude.

Rubin (1983) first conducted an empirical study in Hawaii, USA with her students to gather natural data on uses of the words "thank you" from various people in different situations. She reported that "thank you" could refer not only to gratitude but also to other language functions, such as complimenting or signaling the conclusion of a conversation. Her study also showed that situations which made the subjects feel especially indebted, surprised, or overwhelmed produced a more lengthy speech act.

The most extensive study on expressions of gratitude has been believed to be the one done by Eisenstein and Bodman (1986). They found from their study that the native-English-speaking subjects did not just express the simple function of thanking like "Thank you very much", they also regularly expressed other functions such as complimenting, reassuring, promising to repay, expressing surprise and delight, expressing a lack of necessity or obligation, and so on. They noted that these expressions of gratitude often took place in speech act sets, rather than a solitary speech act. The study also showed that even advanced non-native English speakers exhibited surprisingly poor performance in expressing gratitude in the target language.

In spite of the extensive and valuable work of the above-mentioned studies, they are all Anglo-oriented. The only substantial cross-cultural comparison regarding peoples' different strategies in expressing gratitude that I know of is the one done by Apte (1974). Apte analyzed the usage of gratitude expressions in the Marathi and Hindi speech communities of South Asia and compared it with that in American society. The article concluded that:

In domains where culture norms are dominant, inappropriate use of gratitude expressions may evoke strong negative responses. In situations where such expressions are generally not used, but are not strongly tabooed if they occur, the response to the use of such expressions by a foreigner may simply be one of confusion, mild amusement or skepticism. On the other hand, observing the rules of verbalization of gratitude properly will result in the individual's acceptance into the new culture more readily. (Apte, 1974:87-88)

Regarding Chinese ways of expressing gratitude and appreciation, Kasper and Zhang (1995:7-8) described several events that some overseas students in China observed while contacting Chinese, and commented that it is not so much verbal expressions, but action, that Chinese people often apply to express their appreciative feelings. Also, Chinese do not thank each other in the family or between close friends. Bricky also noted that

Chinese seldom thank their friends, especially for the small things that friends do for each other. Thanking friends can make the relationship feel formal or distant. The excessive use of "thank you" also tends to sound obsequious. (Bricky, 1990:123)

Obviously, little substantive study has been done about the Chinese strategies of responding to favors, still less in cross-cultural contrastive research between speakers of Chinese culture and native English-speaking culture in this respect. This study will start from an ethnographic observation of people's reaction in the Chinese culture, and proceed with the analysis of the answers of a questionnaire obtained from a group of Chinese native speakers, in the hope that a regular set of Chinese strategies can be found out. After that, a group of Americans will be asked with the same series of questions. These answers will be then compared with those of the Chinese speakers. While discussing the similarities and differences in the answers provided by both groups, this paper also hopes to dig out the cultural reasons that may serve to explain the contrasts.

Before going on with the study, I would like to clarify that this paper does not intend to confine its aim to exploring on-the-site expressions of gratitude like the previous researchers did. In order to have a more panoramic view of the two cultures regarding this issue, the paper will investigate what strategies the subject will take in response to the designed favors. This will open up all possibilities of obtaining and analyzing answers of different aspects: whether verbal or non-verbal, simultaneous or repair, responses or non-responses, etc.

3.2　Methodology: Procedures and Limitations

3.2.1　Preliminary study

In order to see the Chinese tradition of dealing with the events benefiting a person, I closely watched and recorded how they reacted when I sent gifts to some of my friends and relatives during the past vacation. In such situations, I took notes of their reactions related to the respective benefits as soon as they were observed, whether during or after the benefited events. I even videotaped a great part of a business opening ceremony so as to investigate what the hosts would do or say in such a formal situation for their guests' gifts and participation. All these are done as a preliminary study. By analyzing these data, and in combination with my personal experience, I composed a questionnaire for a more directional further study.

3.2.2　Design of questionnaire

Through analyzing the preliminary study described above, I found that apart from formal situations such as performing at the business opening ceremony where actors and actresses always expressed explicit thanks, there are still a lot more various Chinese strategies of responding to favors. They may respond to it on the site, or they may respond to it afterwards; they may express their gratitude verbally, they may also do it through action; they may show their thanks directly to the other side, or they may also do it indirectly by complimenting the person who offers a favor before other people. Moreover, they may, in some situations, feel more natural to give no response at all. In order to avoid oversimplified answers from subjects and to obtain a more complete picture of what Chinese would do or say in the relevant situations, I put the above possibilities at the beginning of the questionnaire in Chinese.

As for the situations included in the questionnaire, I used as many of those designed by Eisenstein and Bodman (1986) as possible so that the result may be more comparable with their study. However, I also noticed that some of the situations designed by Eisenstein and Bodman were a little too long and might result in psychological impatience of the subjects and further affect the reliability of their answers. Therefore, I simplified and shortened the ones that I was going to use in the current study. Meanwhile, I felt that I had to replace some of the situations with something more suitable in the Chinese culture or something that would elicit more information-rich answers in the culture. (Please refer to attachment 1).

The English questionnaire is basically a translation of the Chinese version with the exception of the currencies. The same currency of US dollars and the amount as used in Eisenstein and Bodman's situations were adopted in the English questionnaire (Please refer to attachment 2). In the Chinese questionnaire, however, RMB is used instead of US dollars so as to make it easy for our Chinese subjects to better visualize the situations. Nonetheless, the critical thing I realized is that while a certain amount of money is transferred from US dollars into Chinese RMB for the contrastive purposes in this study, people's identical psychological response of the amount in the Chinese culture should be aroused. This is a rather complicated issue since it is related to an extensive number of factors. It means that the currency transference should not be calculated just in accordance with the official exchange rate. Factors such as the average income level of the Chinese in comparison with that of Americans, components of their respective routine expenditure, market prices, etc. should also be put into comprehensive consideration. With the consideration of all such factors, I would assume that every US dollar to average Americans must be psychologically identical to the ordinary contemporary Chinese as 2 *yuan* RMB. For example, an American borrowing 500 US dollars from a friend would arouse a similar indebted feeling as a Chinese borrowing 1,000 *yuan* RMB from his/her friend, this is transferred accordingly in the Chinese version of the questionnaire.

3.2.3 Subjects of the study

34 students in a class of correspondence course in Chinese major studying in a college in Yunnan were chosen as the Chinese subjects of this study. They age from 22 to 37 years old and consist of Han, Naxi and Bai nationalities from Yunnan province. Despite of the participation of a small section of other L1 groups (6 altogether), they were basically brought up in the Chinese culture and their Chinese

proficiency is equal to the Chinese L1 people. There were 5 dropouts, and as a result, 29 answer sheets and 406 answers were collected for analysis.

Only 15 American students of Chinese or American teachers of English in the same college were available to participate in this study. English is the first language for all of these American subjects. Their ages range from 21 to 50 years old and come from either the north or the south of the United States. The English questionnaire was given to them and 13 copies altogether 182 answers were obtained for further comparison with those from the Chinese group.

3.2.4 Limitations and minimization of limitations

As we know, written answers for hypothetical situations are not equal to authentic natural answers. What people think they should do or say may not necessarily be what they would actually do or say in real life. Moreover, as the Chinese subjects speak Chinese with different accents of their own regions and some expressions in their own dialects are different from that of Putonghua, when they are asked to put them down on paper, they are more likely to copy the standard expressions and behavior of the people they learn from various media or novels which they believe to be standard. In order to avoid such coinage or transference from other sources to the greatest extent, before they began to answer the questionnaire, the subjects were reminded not to think of what they believe they ought to say or do in the relevant situations. Instead, they had to imagine they themselves to be personally involved in the situations provided and write down directly what they would intuitively think of doing or saying in their real life. They were encouraged to write down their oral utterances in the closest possible ways as they would take place in their own dialects, including slang. They were also encouraged to use Chinese pinyin to denote the expressions they speak in their own dialects but cannot be matched with any characters they know of in the Chinese writing system. Whatever differences found between their dialects and Chinese Putonghua were noted in brackets following the expressions while summarizing the data collected. Only a few of such differences have been found, in fact.

The same request was made for the American subjects to write down what they would intuitively think of responding to the situations, and avoid thinking really carefully about what they ought to say or do. They were also asked to consider the possibilities of both verbal and non-verbal responses, on-site and postponed responses, verbal comments to the third person as well as to the second person. While writing verbal answers, they were required to record exactly what they would say in their daily life, including slang only their region would use, if any. These requirements were offered to the American subjects as well so that the same conditions for eliciting answers were given to both groups for a fair comparative study.

3.3 Results of the Study and Preliminary Discussion

3.3.1 Responses from American subjects

Although the data from the American subjects were collected last, for the convenience of data description and analysis, I put them before those obtained from the Chinese subjects for interpretations.

In looking at the answers of the Americans to situations 4 (to a cashier), 5 (to a friend who says to a friend at a meal, "You have something on your face."), 10 (to a friend handing over a newspaper), 11 (to a taxi driver), it is clear for us to see, just like what Eisenstein and Bodman found, that one would generally just produce phatic and ritualized responses like: "Thank you" "Thanks" "Thank you. Have a great day" "Thanks. Have a nice day" "Thanks a bunch", etc. To most of the Americans, the expression of thanks in such situations seems to be a social amenity made automatically, whether it was the addressee's job to implement the service or not.

In situations 1, 6, and 8, it has been noted that the speech act set of promising to repay or reciprocate is used with explicit thanking, e.g. "I will pay you back as soon as possible." "I will pay you back when I get home or see you again." "I'll pay you back as soon as I can." "As soon as I get paid, I'll pay you back." "The next time is my turn to buy." "I'll catch you next time."

The function of complimenting is found in situations 2, 3, 9 and 10. For instance, "This is beautiful!" "It's great to have a boss like you." "That was very thoughtful of you." "This is really nice." "You are great parents." "You guys are too great." "Dinner was great!" "I had a great evening and the food was wonderful." "The food and company was great."

Situations 8 and 9 have elicited some good examples when a lack of necessity or obligation is expressed. For example, "You didn't have to do that!" "You didn't have to pay!" "You did not have to do this." "Y'all know y'all didn't have to."

Expressions of surprise and delight can be spotted in situations 2 and 3, such as, "Wow!" "Oh!" "Great!" "Oh wow!" "What a wonderful surprise."

As indicated in situation 7, orally expressing affection with intimate terms seems to be a rather useful American strategy used between intimate people like spouses to show their gratitude. E.g. "...honey! That was so sweet of you!" "Oh babe..." "..., sweetie. You're a real doll..." "Oh! Honey, I love you." "You are a sweetheart."

3.3.2 Responses from Chinese subjects

3.3.2.1 Verbal strategies

From the answers supplied by the Chinese respondents, it was found that they also used many identical verbal strategies applied by the native English-speaking Americans.

These are:

1. Explicit thanking such as, "xiexie" (Thanks), "xiexie ni" (Thank you), "duoxie" (Many thanks), or "xiexie nide guanxin" (Thank you for your concerns) (in situations 1, 3, 10 and 11);

2. Promising to repay or reciprocate, for instance, "wo mingtian huan ni" (I will return it to you tomorrow) (for situation 1), "yiyouqian, wo mashang huan ni" (I will refund you as soon as I have that amount of money) and "guo jitian wo yiding huan ni" (I'll be sure to refund you in just a few days) (for situation 6), also "xiahui wo qing ni" (Next time is on me) (for situation 8);

3. Complimenting, e.g. "ya, zhemeduo haochide" (Alas, you have brought so much tasty food) (for situation 9), "ni zhenshi wode hao laogong" (You are really my good husband) (for situation 7), "zhejian yifu tai piaoliang le" (This coat is so pretty) (for situation 2);

4. Expressing surprise and delight, such as "tai chuhu yiliao le" (It was really out of my expectation), "a" (Ah), (for situations 7 and 8), "wo, tai xingfu le" (Oh, I'm so happy) (for situation 2);

5. Expressing a lack of necessity or obligation, for instance, "bubi name pofei ma" (You didn't have to spend so much money) (for situation 2), "buyong laofan

(mafan) lema" (You didn't have to trouble to do it for me) (for situation 13). In spite of the application of the same strategies in expressing gratitude as described above, the Chinese students used strategies 1, 3 and 4 far less frequently than Americans, thus are not typical strategies applied by the Chinese subjects (please refer to the chart over-leaf).

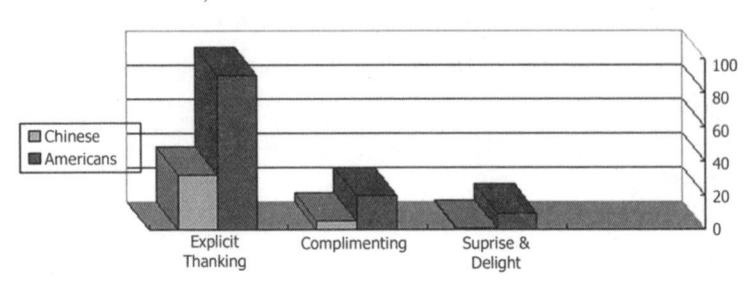

Note: Since we did not have equal numbers of Chinese and American subjects, we had to use percentages instead of raw numbers to make the comparison between the two groups. First, all the expressions where each of the strategies was applied in the answers to all the 14 situations were counted respectively. The proportion of each of these numbers in the total answers of each group (406 answers from the Chinese subjects and 182 from the Americans) was then indicated in the form of percentage (The vertical number).

In comparison with the answers obtained from the American subjects, more typical Chinese strategies of expressing gratitude have been found to include ritualized refusal, positive blaming, expressing embarrassment, acknowledging trouble or expenditure, and parade before a third person.

In the strategy of ritualized refusal, Chinese subjects would practice a series of refusal to show their traditional courtesy before accepting an offer, e.g. "buyong" (Not necessary), or "buxu duoli" (Don't you need to be so courteous) in situation 2, "buxiao (buyong) zheme mafan le" (Don't go to so much trouble) in situation 9. Several Chinese subjects agreed that it is important to practice a process of ritual refusal to a friendly offer at the beginning, or people would feel that the offer is belittled.

In the case of positive blaming, the subject feels quite indebted about the expenses and trouble one went into for the gifts, and would pretend to blame the supplier about it. For instance, some subjects would "blame" a friend who sent him/her a gift on his/her birthday (situation 2), "ni bugai mai zheme guizhong de liwu" (You shouldn't have bought such an expensive gift for me), "ganma hai songgei wo liwu ne?" (Why should you give me gift at all?); another subject would say to her parents who came to see her with a lot of foodstuff (situation 9), "zenme dailai zhemeduo dongxi? Yihou buneng zhemezuo le" (Why did you bring so much stuff? You shouldn't do it anymore in the future). As shown in the last example, a "warning" of not repeating the same practice in the future could be added to emphasize the effect as well.

Expressing embarrassment has been noticed to be a rather applicable strategy in many different situations for Chinese speakers. Instances of such expression are found in situations1, 2, 5 , 6, 7, 12, 13, and 14, such as "buhao yisi le" (I feel embarrassed about it), "zhende buhao yisi" (I feel quite embarrassed for it), and "rang ni pofei zhenshi buhao yisi" (It's really embarrassing that you spent money for me), etc.

The strategy of acknowledging the trouble or expenditure that one has caused to the other side appears to be a fairly acceptable practice for Chinese, too. To a friend who sent her a pretty coat on her birthday (situation 2), a subject responded, "rang ni pofei le" (I have caused you to spend money). Some subjects would say to a friend who was seeing him/her off from a dinner (situation 12), "gei nimen tian mafan le" (I have increased your trouble), "tai mafan ni le" (I have troubled you a lot), or "jingtian darao le" (We have interrupted you today). This strategy can be commonly used as a phatic or ritualized way of thanking, e.g. one may say to a taxi driver or cashier, "mafan ni" (I have troubled you), "mafan le" (I have caused trouble). Such expressions are often used as a substitution for "xiexie" (Thanks), or "xiexie ni" (Thank you).

In many situations, the Chinese subjects would show their positive feelings for the gift or the corresponding person to a third person as an important supplemental expression of gratitude. For example, in situation 2, three subjects explained that after they had accepted the coat with compliments, they would also parade the gift to other people and express their love for it. Instead of complimenting the object or person directly in the presence of the corresponding person, the subjects sometimes feel more comfortable to compliment them only before the third person. For instance, in situation 3, three subjects would rather say something in favor of their boss with other people instead of thanking or flattering him/her face to face. They explained that paying compliments directly to the corresponding person is often considered apple-polishing or shallow, and is thus despised. Whereas, spreading favorable words about somebody can add to his/her good reputation and it is very important to establish a good reputation for someone you like. Therefore, by doing so, they would feel some relief from indebtedness.

3.3.2.2 Non-verbalization of gratitude

There are two kinds of this non-verbalization: unnecessary verbalization of gratitude, and actualization of returning cherished gratitude.

By comparing the results from both of the groups, one would instantly find that the Chinese subjects tend not to verbalize gratitude in certain situations when they feel it unnecessary to. For instance, many of them do not feel it necessary to thank the taxi driver or supermarket cashier as they think it their work or responsibility to serve them with payment. Also, many of them would not verbally thank their parents, spouses or intimate friends for anything they do for them. However, it does not necessarily mean that they do not feel indebtedness. In many cases, they just think that verbalization of gratitude alone would sound shallow and meaningless to good friends. They will cherish the gratitude in the mind and seek for opportunities to show their thanks through actions. For example, in response to situation 8, none of the subjects would explicitly verbalize his/her thanks to a good friend who invited him/her for meal. 25 out of all the 29 subjects would rather treat him/her for a meal or something else another time instead of verbal thanking. For situation 9, half of the subjects think that they would keep their parents' love in their mind and show their gratitude by treating them well, buying gifts for them, or show their filial piety to them through various actions.

3.4 Cross-Cultural Discussion

3.4.1 Implicitness and explicitness

Means of expressing feelings are very different between Chinese and Western peoples. Wang and Li (1993) noted that the Chinese implicitness forms the basis of the traditional Chinese thinking style. Lu (2000) also observed that Westerners often express what they feel openly and explicitly, while Chinese like to suggest their feelings implicitly and love the mood of "cishi wusheng sheng yousheng" (Silence speaks louder than voice). Westerners cannot understand why Chinese should express their feelings through various hints and consider it a beauty while they could very well expose their mind thoroughly with no effort at all. Meanwhile, Chinese often cannot bear the shallowness of explicit expression of inner world without considering concrete conditions.

From the current study, it is clear for us to see that the English-speaking subjects always tried their utmost to express their gratitude to the greatest possible extent explicitly and simultaneously to the corresponding person. However, the Chinese respondents were not found to be very much in favor of explicit expression of gratitude. They would often take to various implicit strategies like ritualized refusal, positive blaming, expressing embarrassment, expression of trouble or expenditure, and parade before the third person, etc., as were discussed in the previous section. In fact, 90.7 percent of all the answers from the Americans contain explicit expressions of gratitude, while only 31.9 percent of the answers from the Chinese include such explicit expressions.

3.4.2 Inner feelings and utilitarianism

Traditionally, Chinese think that one is obliged to "exchange heart with heart" with the person who is kind to him/her, or he/she would be regarded heartless (Sun:1987). While analyzing the Sino-Western cultural differences, Yu (1984) pointed out three major distinctions, one of which is that Chinese culture is an introversive culture and underlines intrinsic excelling, while Western culture belongs to an extroversive culture and stresses extrinsic excelling. Lu (2000) also commented that Westerners value benefit but belittle innermost feelings, while Orientals often emphasize innermost feelings more than benefit or emphasize both equally. In other words, Chinese often consider what "I' feel about something, and many Westerners often think about what something can actually bring to me" :friendship or money? This might explain why many Chinese subjects described in their answers what they would feel about a situation, what they should do to make themselves feel better without considering much about its utilitarian function; this might also explain why the American subjects seemed to care more about what they said to the other side had exhausted their appreciative feelings right there and then. Talking about this reminds me of a Chinese who gave up an opportunity of earning several hundred dollars a day for one week just to help one of his good friends around the town doing some small business, and he never let his friend know about it.

3.4.3 Equality and social distance

Americans believe the saying that "all men are born equal". They try every effort to ensure that everybody be treated equally and fairly. However, people in China are basically treated differently according to seniority, social status and social distance. This value must have some fundamental reflection in their different strategies of expressing gratitude as well. As shown in the current study, expressions of gratitude used by Americans and their inner feelings seem to have shown very little difference from person to person, no matter whom they are directed to: whether old or young, whether they are strangers, friends, parents, spouses or leaders. But to Chinese, how favor is responded to is a significant clue of identifying social distance. They rarely express explicit thanks to their family members or very intimate friends as it is considered a formality only needed in dealing with "outsiders". As one of the Chinese subjects put it, "The more you show your gratitude openly, the more you appear distant from the person you speak to. Why do close friends have to be that ceremonious?"

Meanwhile, it is interesting to notice that the Chinese subjects regard highly of whatever their old parents do for them. Even trivial things like adding some rice for them (situation 13) would result in great indebted feelings. One subject described that she would stand up to reach for the rice bowl with two hands and say, "You didn't have to do that for me." A few other Chinese subjects would refuse to allow their parents to do it for them. During the interview, some of the Chinese admitted that they would respond entirely differently if it were their children who did it for them, they would just take it for granted. This might be related to the traditional Chinese filial piety for parents.

3.4.4 Speech and action

It is impossible to find the roots for the Chinese culture without mentioning Confucius. Confucius advocated that integrity and action should always be performed before speech; integrity and action takes the lead and good speech will follow (Cai, 1993). The Chinese traditional love for integrity and action and hatred for deceitful eloquence must have resulted in an extremity of overlooking the importance of good speech. As indicated in the current study, Chinese appear a lot more dependant on follow-up actions than Americans in expressing their gratitude. Many Chinese subjects responded to situation 3 that they would work hard to return the boss' favor of increasing their salary; some of them even claimed that they would not say anything to thank their boss, but they would keep on working hard or even harder than before. However, all of the American subjects expressed their thanks very well before the boss, but only one of them remembered to make a statement that he/she would continue to work hard.

A very interesting finding related to this issue is that while the Americans almost always make a more lengthy speech act set in the situations which made them feel especially indebted, surprised, or overwhelmed, as was found by Rubin (1983), Eisenstein and Bodman (1986), this is not obvious to the Chinese subjects. However, in such situations, they did think more to return the favor through action.

3.5 Conclusion

This paper has compared the strategies applied by Chinese and Americans in response to favors. The typical strategies of expressing gratitude used by Americans are found to be more explicit, immediate and more verbal-oriented. They generally combine their explicit thanking with other speech act sets such as: promising to repay or reciprocate, complimenting, expression of a lack of necessity or obligation, expression of surprise and delight, and expression of affection, etc. The same set of strategies is also found among the Chinese subjects. However, the Chinese subjects than the American subjects use explicit thanking, complimenting, expression of surprise and delight, and expression of affection far less frequently. Other than promising to repay or reciprocate, expression of a lack of necessity or obligation, a traditional set of verbal strategies that the Chinese use are found to be ritualized refusal, positive blaming, expressing embarrassment, expression of notice for trouble or expenditure, and parade before the third person, etc. As a whole, it has been found that the Chinese strategies of responding to favors are rather implicit and action-oriented.

To Chinese, unlike Americans, how much effort one takes in expressing explicit thanks often shows their social distance with the other side; The more one shows his/her overt gratitude, the more he/she appears relationally distant from the person he/she speaks to. This study has also found that the Chinese subjects do not necessarily produce a more lengthy speech act set like Americans generally do, in the situations which made them feel especially indebted, surprised, or overwhelmed. But they thought more about returning the favors through future actions.

To compare with Americans, Chinese appear to consider less about utilitarian function of their speech or action; they often tend to concentrate more on balancing their innermost feelings than showing to the other side how much they feel about the favors.

References:

Apte M. L. "Thank you" and South Asian Languages: A Comparative Sociolinguistics Study. International Journal of the Sociology of Language, 1974(3): 67-89.

Bricky J. China: A Handbook in International Communication. Sydney: NCELTR, 1990.

Cai, Yushu. Kongzi yuyanguan gailun: xia (Outline for Language Concepts of Confucius: Topic 2). Journal of Yunnan Institute of Minorities: Social science volume, 1993: 77-82.

Eisenstein, M. and Bodman. J. W. I Very Appreciate: Expressions of Gratitude by Native and Non-native Speakers of American English. Applied Linguistics. Oxford University Press, 1986(2/7): 166-183.

Kasper, G. and Zhang Yanyin Thanking and Appreciation. Pragmatics of Chinese as Native and Target Language. Second Language & Curriculum Center. University of Hawaii at Manoa, 1995.

Leech, G. N. Pinciples of Pragmatics. London: Longman, 1983.

Lu, Qiutian. Different Styles of Thinking between East and West. Readers, 2000 (9): 38-40.

Rubin, J. The Use of "Thank You". Paper presented at the Socio-linguistics Colloquium, TESOL Convention, Toronto, Canada, 1983.

Searle, J. R. Speech Acts: An Essay in the Philosophy of Language. Cambridge: Cambridge University Press, 1969.

Wang, Moxi, Li Jin. A study on English discourse thinking mode of Chinese students.Foreign Language Teaching and research,1993(4):64.

Yu, Shiying. Viewing Contemporary Meanings of Chinese Culture through Its Value System. Taiwan Cultural Publishing Corporation,1984.

Appendix I Questionnaire for Americans

Please read the following short descriptions of situations in which you are involved. Consider how you might respond to the respective situations. You might say something to the other side on the spot; or you might choose to say something to the other side afterwards; or you might choose to say something to some other people instead; or you might want to express your feelings to the other side non-verbally instead of verbal means (e.g. Pay for the meal next time when we eat together.). Of course, in some situation, you might find it better to respond in more than one of the means described above, or perhaps you might feel it unnecessary to respond in any means at all. Write your response (if any) in the space provided. Please quote all the verbal responses and indicate the situation you say it (e.g. On the spot: "Thank you very much."). If you choose not to respond in any means at all, please put a cross in the space. Would you consider these suggestions while you write your responses to the situations? 1. Use the kind of language you find most natural, including slang that you are used to speaking if any. 2. Try not to consider what you should do or say, but what you think you would intuitively do or say in the respective situations. Thank you very much for your time and sincerity!

Situation 1. You go shopping with your friend. When he/she heard that you have not brought enough money, he/she said, "I have got plenty. How much do you need?" You say, "Could you lend me $5.00?" Your friend says, "Are you sure $5.00 is enough for you?" You say it is enough and your friend gives you the $5.00.

Situation 2. It's your birthday, and you're having a few people over for dinner. A friend brings a pretty coat for you as gift.

Situation 3. You have been working for a large company for 6 months. One day, your boss calls you into his/her office.

Situation 4. In the supermarket, the cashier puts your groceries in bags and turns to begin checking out the next customer. You pick up your bags to leave.

Situation 5. At the table in a restaurant a friend says, "You have something on your face." You ask where. Your friend tells you. You rub your face and ask, "Is it off?" Your friend says that it is.

Situation 6. You find yourself in bad need of $500.00. You mention this to a good friend of yours. He/she immediately offers to lend it to you and hands the $500.00 to you right away. You take the money gratefully.

Situation 7. You are married. Both you and your spouse work. You come home late from work and find that your spouse has done some work around the house that you had promised to do but had not a chance to do.

Situation 8. Your good friend invites you to eat out. He/she pays after you have finished the meal.

Situation 9. Now you have got a job and are on your own. Your parents come to visit you. They have brought along a lot of foodstuff for you as gifts.

Situation 10. You are sharing an apartment with a friend. You are both sitting and relaxing in the living room. You ask your friend to hand you the newspaper which is nearby. Your friend gives you the newspaper.

Situation11. You go to a park by a taxi. You give the driver money according to the amount shown on the meter as you get off from the taxi.

Situation 12. You have been invited to the home of a rather new friend. You have dinner with him/her and his/her spouse and a few other friends of theirs. The food was great, and you really enjoyed the evening. As you leave, your hosts accompany you to the door.

Situation 13. You are eating with your family at home. Your father/mother sees that it is inconvenient for you to add some more rice, he/she gets up and do it for you.

Situation 14. You go to another city to visit a company for your own company. During your stay, the company you visit has treated you warm-heartedly. When you leave, the manager personally sees you off at the bus station.

The following details about you yourself will only be used for the purpose of this research and will be kept confidential; please fill in the blanks accordingly. However, you are also entitled to refuse filling in these blanks if you are unwilling to. Thank you!

Sex_____   Marital status_____   Age_____
Nationality_____   First Language_____

Thank you very much for your cooperation!

Appendix II Answers Obtained from the Questionnaire for Americans

Situation 1.

Appendix II   Answers Obtained from the Questionnaire for Americans "Thank you so much!"

"Man, thanks a bunch, I'll make sure to pay you back once we get to my place." "I'll catch you later."

"I will pay you back as soon as I get to the bank (or home)."

"I very much appreciate you lending me the money. I'll repay you when we get home." "Thanks a lot. I'll pay you back when we get back to my house."

"Thank you, I will pay you back as soon as possible."

"Thank you" . Treat them to something small later, such as a cup of coffee. "Hey, thanks. I'll pay you back as soon as we get back to my house." "Thanks, I'll pay you back tomorrow."

"Thank you very much. I will pay you back when I get home or see you again." "Thank you. I'll pay you back as soon as we get back. "

"Thanks, I appreciate that."

Situation 2.

"Wow! Thank you so much! I love it!" That week, I will write that friend a thank-you note and mail it to her. "Wow! This is beautiful! Thank you so much."

"Wow! Thanks!"

"This is beautiful, thank you."

"What a beautiful coat, I'll enjoy wearing it. Thank you." "It's beautiful. You guys are too much."

"Thank you for the beautiful coat. That was very thoughtful of you." Hug them and say, "Thank you."

"Oh wow! Thank you so much. It's wonderful." "Thank you. I love it."

"Thank you" or "It's great, Thanks."

"Wow! It's beautiful! You shouldn't have gone to such trouble for my birthday. Thank you so much!" "Wow, you shouldn't have, but since you did, thank you very much. Wow, this is really nice."

Situation 3.

"Thank you, sir (man), it's been a pleasure working for you."

"Thank you so much sir. I truly have enjoyed the opportunity to work here and will continue to strive my best."

"Hey! I appreciate that."

"Thank you very much, I can really use the increase." "That's great! I really appreciate it. Thank you."

"Thank you sir (man), It has been a pleasure to work in this company."

"Thank you! I'm glad that you are pleased with my work and I appreciate the raise."

"I appreciate being recognized as a good employee." Make sure that I continue to work hard. "Thank you, sir/ma'am. I appreciate it. Thank you for noticing."

"Thank you. I appreciate that."

"Great! Thank you very much. I appreciate your confidence in me."

"Oh, thank you. It's great to have a boss like you. I appreciate your thoughtfulness." "Well, thank you very much. I am glad that you are pleased with my work."

Situation 4.

"Thank you. Have a nice day." (2) "Thanks." (4)

"Thank you. Have a great day."

"Take it easy!" or "Have a good one" I would use their name if I'm friends with them. "Thank you" or just leave since they are already busy helping someone else. "Thanks" or "Thank you, have a good day."

"See you later, bye."

If she has already begun to check out the next customer, I would not say anything. In fact, I may consider it a little rude if she did not say "thank you" or "goodbye" to which I could respond with the same.

Situation 5.

"Thanks for telling me!" (3)

"Thanks, rather you tell me than somebody else." "Thanks!" (4)

"Thanks so much. I hate it if someone doesn't tell me." "Thank you for telling me."

Verbally express my appreciation by using humor. "Hey, thanks."

"Thanks, I didn't want to look silly all night."

Situation 6.

"Thank you so much! I'll pay you back right away."

"I am very embarrassed about this, but thank you very much. I will be sure to pay you back as soon as I can." "Thanks! I'll pay you when I get the money."

"I realize this is a lot of money and I do appreciate it. I will pay you back as soon as possible. I may only be able to pay you $100/month till it's paid off."

"This means too much to me. I'm so grateful to you. I'll pay you back when my check arrives." "This is a great help, thank you so much. I'll return the money as soon as I can."

"Thank you for taking care of my needs. I will be sure to pay you back as soon as possible."

First, I would avoid borrowing money from a friend. But I would verbally thank them on the spot. I would pay them back as soon as possible & treat them to a nice meal after I paid them back. I would not mention what they did for me again but I would always remember it.

"Are you sure? This won't put you in a bind will it? Ok, then. Thank you so much. I'll get this back to you as soon as possible."

"Thank you for helping, I'll pay you back as soon as I can."

"Thank you." Or "Thanks so much, you're a lifesaver. I'll pay you back as soon as I can." "Thank you so much. I appreciate you helping me out like this. As soon as I get paid, I'll pay you back. OK? Thanks."

"I deeply appreciate this. I will pay you back as soon as possible. I hope it is no trouble for you. Again, thank you."

Situation 7.

"Thanks honey! That was so sweet of you!"

"Oh babe, you are the best. Thank you so much. I owe you one."

"Thanks, dear, you didn't need to do that. But I do appreciate it very much."

"I feel badly that I did not get to this sooner. Thank you for doing it, I got too busy." "What a wonderful surprise. Thank you for helping me."

"Thanks sweetie, you're a real doll to help me."

"The house looks nice! I'm sorry that I hadn't fixed those things that I had promised. But, you did a great job!"

Verbally and physically let her know how much it meant to me. "Thanks honey." And give her a hug and a kiss.

"I'm sorry for not getting it done." Then I will offer to cook dinner for the two of us. "Thanks for doing that, it was a big help."

"Thank you for doing that. I'm sorry I didn't get to it." Or "Thank you, very nice of you to do that, I should have done that."

"Oh! Honey, I love you. Thanks for helping me out. Work has kept me so busy lately." "Sorry I didn't get that done, you're a sweet heart. Thanks for being so understanding."

Situation 8.

"Thanks for the dinner. You really didn't have to do that!" "You didn't have to do that! The next one is on me." "Thanks! I'll catch you next time."

"Thanks so much, next time it's my turn."

"Thank you for the meal and your friendship. I'll treat you next time." "Thanks a lot. I'll catch you next time."

"Thank you for the meal. The next time it is my turn to buy."

"Thanks for picking up the check, (name)." Return the favor at a later date. "Thank you for lunch/dinner. Next time it's my treat."

"Thanks. Next time it's my treat."

"Thank you so much for the meal!" Or "Thank you. The next one is on me. OK?" "Oh! You didn't have to pay, but thank you. Next time let me pay, OK?" "Thanks, (name). That was sure nice of you. Next time is on me."

Situation 9.

"Thanks guys! You shouldn't have!" Write a thank-you note. "Mom, Dad, you guys are too great. I love you."

"Oh, thanks, I can really use this!" "Wow, this will be great, thank you."

"All of the things you brought I can really use. You are great parents. Thank you." "Oh mom & dad, you did not have to do this. Thank you so much."

"Thank you for the food. I'm so glad that you both were able to come and visit me in my new home." "Thanks for bringing the food, y'all know y'all didn't have to." When they leave hug them as you say goodbye and thank them again.

"Mom, Dad, thank you. Let me take you two to dinner as appreciation."

"Thanks, mom/dad."

"Thanks." Or "Why, I am doing fine. You didn't have to do that." "Mom, dad, wow, this is great! Thanks a lot. It feels like home again."

Although on my own, I would still appreciate the fact that they are concerned for me, and tell them so.

Situation 10.

"Thanks." (8)

"Thank you." (2)

"Thanks. (name)." "Thanks man."

Situation 11.

"Thank you." (4)

"Thanks a bunch. Can you come back at 6:00 and pick me up?" "Thanks." (3)

"Have a great day. Thank you." "Thank you, have a nice day!"

"Take it easy!" or "Have a good one." "Thanks. Have a nice day." Or "Thank you." "Bye, thanks."

Situation 12.

"Thank you for such a wonderful evening. Dinner was great!" Later I would invite them over for dinner. "Man, tonight was a great time, let's do this again soon. " Later I would invite them over to return the favor. "The food and company was great. Thanks. I really enjoyed our time together."

"I had a great evening and the food was wonderful. Thank you for inviting me."

"I enjoyed your family and friends this evening, also the great food. Thank you for inviting me over." "Thank you for a wonderful evening. The food and conversation were both 'well-seasoned'."

"Thank you for inviting me over for dinner. The food was great and I had a wonderful time!"

Shake their hand & verbally express my gratitude. Depending on what he/she likes to do invite them fishing, golfing, etc. If a girl or a married couple, send a thank-you note or card.

"Thank you so much for the invitation for dinner. I had a great time." "Thank you, it was a lovely evening."

"Thank you so much for the great meal. We'll have to do it again sometime only next time our house." "Thank you so much for the invite. Dinner was delicious;

you're a great cook. We really enjoyed our evening together. Next time you'll have to come to our place. Thanks, goodbye." "Thank you so much for a wonderful time. We really enjoyed our time with you."

Situation 13.

"Thank you Mom/Dad." (4) "Thanks mom/dad!" (4)

"Oh, thanks mom. You didn't need to do that." "Thanks for your help."

"Thanks for getting the rice."

"Oh, thanks, just a little more please." "Mom, I can get it, don't bother."

Situation 14.

"Thanks for your hospitality. We look forward to working with you." Later I might send him a thank you note.

"Thank you for sending me off, I know that you are a very busy man." "Thanks for your help and hospitality."

"You have treated me well and it was a pleasure to be here. Thank you very much." "Thank you. I appreciate all you have done for me and for taking me to the bus station." "Thank you so much for your hospitality. I have really appreciated your thoughtfulness."

"Thank you for all you have done. I really enjoyed my stay and look forward to working with you again." "Thank you for treating me so well. I will be in touch soon." Write them a note on a very nice card & possibly send a gift with the card.

"I want you to know that I really appreciate how well I've been treated during my stay. It speaks incredibly well of your company and your administration. Thank you."

"Thank you, I really enjoyed my visit."

"Thank you for your great care." Or "Thanks for everything."

"Thanks for your worm hospitality. I'll send your regards to my boss. Bye. Hope we get another chance to do business."

"Thank you, I hope we have the chance to work together again sometime."

Appendix III　Questionnaire for Chinese Subjects

问　卷

请仔细阅读以下各类情景的描述。设想对方在为你做了这些事后,你会做出什么反应? 你可能当场就会跟对方说什么;也可能在事后的某个场合跟对方说什么;或者对别人说什么;也许会用某种非语言方式表达您的心情(如:事后回请他/她一顿饭);也许兼而有之(如,当场说:"当真的? 那就不客气了。"事后回请一顿饭。);还可能什么也不说不做(如果这样,请在相应的位置画"×")。为了保持其原真性,在做出回答时,请注意不要考虑应该怎么说或怎么做才标准,只记录你在相应的日常情况下会怎么反应。在记录语言表达时,请直接使用自己的方言表达方式。不好用汉字表达的地方音可用拼音或同音字代替:

1.你和你的好朋友一块上街买东西,他(她)听到你说没带够钱,当即就说:"我带的多,你要多少?"你说:"借我十块,后天还你。"你的朋友问:"十块真的够不够?"你说够了。你的朋友当场就掏出十块给你。

2.你的生日这天,你邀了几个人来吃饭。一个朋友给你带来一件漂亮的衣服做礼物。

3.你在一家大公司工作六个月后,老板叫你到他(她)的办公室并告诉你:"你干得不错,我们对你的工作很满意。我决定给你每月加薪150块。"

4.你在超市收银台付款后,营业员将你的东西放入袋中递给你,转身给另一位顾客算账。

5.在餐厅吃饭时,一个朋友告诉你:"你的脸上粘着一点儿东西。"你问他(她)在那里。他(她)告诉了你。你揩了揩,问道:"还有没有?"他(她)说没有了。

6.你急需一千元人民币。跟你的好朋友说起这件事后,他(她)马上就表示他(她)可以借给你并当场将钱如数点了给你。你很吃惊也很感激。推迟了一会儿后,你才接了下来。

7.你结了婚。你爱人和你都有工作。你回家后发现他(她)已经将你原来答应要做而又没时间的家务做好了。

8.你的好朋友请你出去吃饭。吃完饭后,他(她)主动付了款。

9.你参加工作后,你父母亲特意赶来看你,来的时候给你带了很多东西。

10.你和你的朋友同住一套房间,你们正坐在客厅休息,你请他(她)将在他(她)身边的一份报纸递给你。你的朋友把报纸递了给你。

11.你打了一辆出租车去公园游玩,下车时,你按所显示的价格把钱给了他(她)。

12.你被邀请到一位刚认识的新朋友家吃饭。你跟他(她),他(她)的爱人和他们的其他朋友一块吃饭。饭菜做得很不错,你很开心。你走的时侯。主人还把你送到了大门口。

13.在一家人吃饭的时候,你的母亲(父亲)看到你起来添饭不方便,就起身帮你添了一碗。

14.你因公到另一城市考察,其间你走访的单位对你进行了热情接待。临走时,该单位的负责人将你亲自送到了车站。

你以下的个人情况仅作为研究之用,将给予保密,请如实填写。但如不愿意告知,您亦有权拒绝填写:

性别_____   年龄_____   婚否_____
民族_____   母语_____

Appendix IV
English Translation Version of Questionnaire for Chinese Subjects

Please read the following situations carefully and imagine that someone has done something for you as described, how would you respond to it? You might say something to the other side right on the spot; you might choose to say something to the other side sometime afterwards; you might also choose to say something to someone else instead; you might as well decide to respond non-verbally instead of verbal means (e.g. Pay for the meal next time when we get together.); or sometimes you might find it better to respond in more than one of the means described above; or else you may find it unnecessary to respond in any means at all (in this case, please put a cross "×" in the space). In order to keep the authenticity of your answers to the greatest possible extent, please do not think so much of what you should say or do to keep up with the standards, just think of how you think you would intuitively do or say in the respective situations. Also, please write down your verbal responses directly with the expressions used in the dialect branch of Chinese you speak. You can use other characters of the same pronunciation or pinyin to denote the characters which you cannot find in Putonghua.

Situation 1. You go shopping with your friend. When he/she heard that you have not brought enough money, he/she said, "I have got plenty. How much do you need?" You say, "Could you lend me 10 *yuan*?" Your friend says, "Are you sure 10 *yuan* is enough for you?" You say it is enough and your friend gives you the 10 *yuan* RMB.

Situation 2. It's your birthday, and you're having a few people over for dinner. A friend brings a pretty coat for you as gift.

Situation 3. You have been working for a large company for 6 months. One day, your boss calls you into his/her office and says, "You're doing a good job. In fact, we are so pleased with your work that I'm going to give you a 150 *yuan* a month raise."

Situation 4. In the supermarket, the cashier puts your groceries in bags and turns to begin checking out the next customer. You pick up your bags to leave.

Situation 5. At the table in a restaurant a friend says, "You have something on your face." You ask where. Your friend tells you. You rub your face and ask, "Is it off?" Your friend says that it is.

Situation 6. You find yourself in bad need of 1000 *yuan*. You mention this to a good friend of yours. He/she immediately offers to lend it to you and hands the 1000 *yuan* to you right away. You take the money gratefully.

Situation 7. You are married. Both you and your spouse work. You come home late from work and find that your spouse has done some work around the house that you had promised to do but had not a chance to do.

Situation 8. Your good friend invites you to eat out. He/She pays after you have finished the meal.

Situation 9. Now you have got a job and are on your own. Your parents come to visit you. They have brought along a lot of foodstuff for you as gifts.

Situation 10. You are sharing an apartment with a friend. You are both sitting and relaxing in the living room. You ask your friend to hand you the newspaper which is nearby. Your friend gives you the newspaper.

Situation11. You go to a park by a taxi. You give the driver the money according to the amount shown on the meter as you get off from the taxi.

Situation 12. You have been invited to the home of a rather new friend. You have dinner with him/her and his/her spouse and a few other friends of theirs. The food was great, and you really enjoyed the evening. As you leave, your hosts accompany you to the door.

Situation 13. You are eating with your family at home. Your father/mother sees that it is inconvenient for you to add some more rice, he/she gets up and do it for you.

Situation 14. You go to another city to visit a company for your own company. During your stay, the company you visit has treated you warm-heartedly. When you leave, the manager personally sees you off at the bus station.

The following details about you yourself will only be used for the purpose of this research and will be kept confidential; please fill in the blanks accordingly.

However, you are also entitled to refuse filling in these blanks if you feel unwilling to. Thank you!

    Sex _____   Marital status _____   Age _____

    Nationality _____   First language _____

    Thank you very much for your cooperation!

Appendix V
Answers Obtained from Questionnaire for Chinese Subjects
(With English Translation)

Notes:

1. The italicized words under the Chinese original stand for the word-for-word translation of oral answers.

2. Complete translation of both oral part and descriptive part is directly under the italicized word-for- word translation.

3. In the case that the modified translation is no different from the word for word translation, the latter is omitted.

Situation 1

"谢谢，那我先用啦！"

Thanks then I first use it. "Thanks, I will take it then."

"谢谢您的帮助。" Thank your help. "Thanks for your help."

归还时说："谢谢您的帮助"

Thank your help.

Say while paying back the money, "Thanks for your help."

"不客气了。"

No ceremony.

"I will not stand on ceremony then."

寻找机会报答。

Be always watchful for opportunities to pay back the favor.

"不好意思了"

Feel shameful.

"I feel shameful about it."

对别人说："那天上街,幸好朋友借我20元,不然我就买不成这件东西了。"

That day in the street, fortunate friend lent me 20 *yuan*, or I could not buy the thing.

Say to other people, "It was fortunate that my friend lent me 20 *yuan* that day when I was in the street. Otherwise, I wouldn't be able to buy this thing."

"当真的？不客气了。"

Really no ceremony

"Really? I will not stand on ceremony then."

"回恪(去)了还给你。"

Back go give you.

"I'll give it back to you when I go back".

"等一会儿还给你戛(好吗)。"

Wait a while back give to you.

"I'll give it back to you after a while."

归还时说："谢谢你。"

Thank you.

Say while paying it back, "Thank you."

"多谢。"

"Many thanks."

归还时说："谢谢。"

Thanks.

Say while paying it back, "Thank you."

"谢谢。"

"Thanks."

"谢谢你。"

"Thanks."

"多谢了。到后天就还你,好吗？"还时说："谢谢了。"对方需要时给予帮助。

Many thanks, to the day after tomorrow return to you, OK? Thanks.

"Many thanks. I will give it back to you the day after tomorrow, OK?" Say while returning the money, "Thanks." Provide help whenever the other side needs it.

"谢谢,我明天还你。"

Thanks. I tomorrow return to you. "Thanks. I will return it to you tomorrow."

"什么时候见面又还你。"

Some time meet return to you.

"I will return it to you when I meet you sometime afterwards."

Situation 2

"不用那么客气。"过后说，"我很喜欢你送的东西。"对方生日时送还礼物。

No need that formal. I very like you sent thing.

"You should not have stood on ceremony like that." Say afterwards, "I like the gift you gave me very much". Send the other side a gift on his/her birthday.

"你太认真了，不必那么破费。"

You are too serious. No need to be that extravagant.

"You are too serious. You didn't need to waste so much money."

"您不该买这么贵重的礼物。"

You shouldn't buy so expensive gift.

"You shouldn't have bought such an expensive gift for me."

"不须多礼。"对方生日那天送一礼物。

No need much courtesy.

"Don't you be so courteous. " Send a gift to him/her on his/her birthday.

对方生日那天回赠礼物。

Send him/her a gift on his/her birthday.

"谢谢了！"

"Thanks."

"真漂亮，太谢谢你了。"对别人说："这件衣服是某某朋友送给我的。"到他生日时回送一件价值相当的礼物。

Really pretty, very thank you.This coat is so-and-so friend sent me.

"It's really pretty, thank you very much." Say to other people, "This coat is a gift from my friend so- and-so." Send him/her a gift of the equal value on his/her birthday.

"谢谢了！"对方生日时送一件更好的东西。

"Thanks！" Send him/her a better gift on his/her birthday.

"谢谢,这件衣服我很喜欢。" Thanks this coat I very like. "Thanks, I like this coat very much."

"谢谢,你太好了。" Thanks, you too good. "Thanks, you are so kind."

Section B-Theories and Practice：Exploring Creative TEFL Methodology in the Chinese Context

"我很喜欢这件衣服。"对别人说："这是某某送给我的衣服。"经常穿这件衣服。

I very like this piece of coat. This is so-and-so sent me coat.

"I like this coat very much." Say to other people, "This is a coat as a gift from so-and-so." Often wear this coat.

"不用了。真不好意思。干嘛还送给我礼物呢?"在别人面前夸耀。

No need. Really shameful. Why still send me gift?

"Not necessary. I really feel embarrassed. Why should you give me gift at all?" Parade it before other people.

"谢谢你。这件衣服太漂亮了。"Thank you. This coat is too pretty. "Thank you. This coat is really pretty."

"谢谢你,让你破费了,何必买东西呢?"事后恰当时买一样东西送她。

Thank you, let you spend money, why buy thing?

"Thank you. I have caused you to spend money. What's the need to buy a gift for me?" Buy her a gift sometime afterwards.

"谢谢,这件衣服我非常喜欢。"事后恰当时买一样东西送她。

Thanks, this coat I very like.

"Thanks, I like this coat very much." Send her a gift afterwards in a proper situation.

"这件衣服太漂亮了,让你破费真是不好意思。"等他(她)过生日时回赠一样东西。

This coat is too pretty, let you spend money really is embarrassing.

"This coat is really pretty. It's really embarrassing that you spend money for me." Send him/her a gift on his/her birthday.

"谢谢!"事后恰当时买一样东西送她。

"Thanks!" Buy her a gift afterwards.

"真漂亮,谢谢。"

"Really pretty, thanks."

"太漂亮了。"对别人说:"是某某人给我的,我太喜欢穿了。"常穿这件衣服。

Too pretty. Is so-and-so person gave to me, I too like wearing.

"Very pretty." Say to other people, "This is a gift from so-and-so. I like wearing it very much." Often wear this coat.

"这件衣服太漂亮了,我很喜欢。"

This coat too pretty, I very like.

Section B Theories and Practice: Exploring Creative TEFL Methodology in the Chinese Context

"This coat is so pretty. I like it very much."

"谢谢你。"等他(她)过生日时回赠一样东西。

"Thank you." Send him/her on his/her birthday.

惊喜状:"奥,太幸福了。"常穿这件衣服。

Oh, too happy.

Happily, "Oh, I'm so happy." Often wear this coat.

"谢谢,这件衣服非常适合我。"

Thanks, this coat very suits me.

"Thanks. This coat is very suitable for me."

"你太客气了。"等他(她)过生日时回赠一样东西。

You too much stand on ceremony.

"You are too ceremonious." Send him/her a gift on his/her birthday.

Situation 3

"谢谢你肯定我的成绩。"加倍努力。

Thank you to affirm my achievement.

"Thank you for seeing my contribution to work." Work a lot harder still.

努力工作。

Work hard.

"谢谢上司的重视,我一定加倍努力将工作做得更好。"

Thank boss for recognition. I sure double hard, to make work do better.

"Thank you for thinking highly of me, boss. I will make sure to work much harder and better than before."

"谢谢总经理栽培。"把工作做得更好。

Thank G.M. planting.

"Thank you for nursing me, general manager." Work better than before.

"你太客气了,谢谢你了!"

You too stand on ceremony, thank you. "You are too ceremonious. Thank you."

"谢谢,我一定更加努力的工作。"要在实际行动中证实,工作更努力。

Thanks, I sure much harder work.

"Thanks, I'll be sure to work even harder." Display even harder work in the actual practice.

会更努力地去工作。

I will work harder than before.

"谢谢老板,我会更加努力。"

· 139 ·

Thank boss, I will harder effort.

"Thank you, boss, I'll work even harder."

"谢谢老板。"

Thank boss. "Thank you, boss."

"谢谢你的鼓励,我会继续努力的。"

Thank your encouragement, I will continue to be hard.

"Thank you for your encouragement, I will continue working hard."

"谢谢,我会更加努力的工作。"

Thanks, I will even harder work.

"Thanks, I'll work even harder than before."

"谢谢你的关心,我会继续努力的。"以后工作更卖力。

Thank your concerns, I'll continue hard work.

"Thank you for your concerns, I'll continue working hard." Work even harder later on.

"谢谢,我会努力。"

"Thanks, I will do my best."

"谢谢老板,我会努力干好自己的工作。"好好干工作,回报老板的信任。

Thank boss, I will hard do well own work.

"Thank you, boss. I'll do my best in my work." Work well to return the trust of my boss.

"这是我应该做的。"事后加倍努力工作。

This is I should do.

"It's my duty to work well." Work much harder than before.

对别人说起这件事。

Mention this raise of salary to other people.

"真的吗? 太好了!" Really? Too good. "Really? That's terrific."

事后加倍努力工作,回报老板的重用。

Work harder afterwards to return my boss' recognition.

对别人说老板的好。

Mention the kindness of the boss to other people.

"谢谢您的赏识。"

Thank your appreciation.

"Thank you for your appreciation."

"你能肯定我的工作,我非常感谢。"

You can affirm my work, I very appreciate.

"I really appreciate that you could affirm the achievement of my work."

"承蒙赏识,谢谢。"

Indebted for appreciation, thanks.

"I feel indebted that you appreciate my work so much. Thanks."

和以往一样努力工作。

Work as hard as before.

"谢谢老板,做好工作是我分内的事。"加倍努力工作。

Thank boss, do well work is my duty thing.

"Thank you, boss, it's my duty to do my work well." Work much harder than before.

他早就应该肯定我的成绩。

He should have affirmed my work achievement a lot earlier.

Situation 4

"谢谢。"

"Thanks."

向他点头表示感谢。

Nod at him to show my appreciation.

对他的印象太坏了,下次去别的地方买。

He has given me a bad impression. I'll choose another place for shopping next time.

"麻烦你了。"

Troubled you.

"I have troubled you, haven't I?"

现在的收银员态度真差!

Cashiers nowadays are really bad mannered!

Situation 5

"你帮我再看看,擦干净了没有。"

You help me again look, wiped up or not.

"Take another look for me please. Has it been wiped up already?"

"谢谢你的提醒。"

Thank your reminding "Thanks for telling me."

我会感到不好意思。

I would just feel embarrassed.

过后对对方说："那天幸好你及时告诉我,不然要出洋相了。"

That day fortunate you in time told me, or would have made a show of myself.

Say to the other side afterwards, "It was lucky that you told me about it the other day, or I would have made a show of myself."

"太狼狈了。"

Too discomposed.

"I really look ugly with that."

"谢谢。"

"Thanks."

"谢谢。真不好意思。" Thanks. Really embarrassing. "Thanks. It's really embarrassing."

"谢谢你的提醒,要不然真的要出洋相了。"

Thank for your telling, or really would make a show of myself. Thanks for your telling me, or I would have made a show of myself.

微微一笑,返回原状。

Smile slightly and return to the previous state.

Situation 6

"过几天我一定还你。"

Over several days I'll sure refund you.

"I'll be sure to refund you in just a few days."

"一有钱,我马上还你"

As soon as have money, I immediately refund you. "I will refund you as soon as I have that amount."

"谢谢你的帮助。"尽量早日归还。

Thank your help.

"Thanks for your help." I'll do the best of my abilities to refund him/her as soon as possible.

"谢谢你的帮助。"尽早归还。

Thank your help.

"Thanks for your help." Refund him/her as soon as possible.

心存感激,寻机回报。

I'll keep the appreciation in my heart and seek for opportunities to return the benefaction.

"谢谢。"过后："多亏你借了我钱,我的事情才得以及时解决。"

Thanks. Luckily you lent me money, my problem could be immediately solved.

"Thanks." After that, I would say, "Thanks to your lending me the money, I could solve my problem promptly."

"谢谢。"记在心中。

"Thanks." Remember it in my heart.

"那就谢谢了。"

Then thanks.

"I'll just take it with thanks then."

"过不久我就还你。"从心里感激他。

Over some time I will refund you.

"I'll refund you after some time." I would appreciate him from the bottom of my heart.

"真不好意思。我不久一定想办法还你。谢谢你了。"

Really embarrassing. I soon sure find a way to refund you. Thank you. "I'm really embarrassed. I'll try my best to refund you soon. Thank you."

"真是太感谢你了,在这困难时你拉了我一把。"对方困难时,热心地去帮助他(她)。

Really too thank you, when this difficult you pull me out.

"Thank you very much indeed. You have pulled me out of the difficult situation." I would help him/her warm-heartedly when he/she is in trouble.

"真不好意思,太谢谢你了!"及时还钱,将此情记在心中。

Really embarrassing, too thank you.

"I'm really embarrassed. Thank you very much." Refund the money in time and always remember this favor in my heart.

"谢谢。"还钱时,请对方吃一顿饭,或买一件小礼物送对方。

"Thanks." I would invite him/her for a meal or buy him/her a little gift when I refund him the money.

"谢谢。"跟别人谈起对方的热情帮助。

"Thanks." Mention his/her warm-hearted help before other people.

过后说:"真是太谢谢你了,解了我的燃眉之急;以后有帮得上的地方,一定尽力而为。"

Really very thank you. Relieved my immediate urgency. Later have help possible areas, sure do my best.

Say afterwards, "Thank you very much indeed. You relieved me from the extremely urgent need. If you come across some situations where I can be of help, I'll do my best for sure."

"谢谢,我很快就还你。" Thanks, I soon will refund you. "Thanks, I will soon refund you."

"谢谢你。"过后请对方吃一顿。

"Thank you." Invite him/her to have a meal later on.

偿还并记住恩情。

Refund him/her and remember the benefaction.

对方困难时,热心地去帮助他(她)。

Help him/her warm-heartedly when he/she is in difficulty.

方便时请吃饭或送她的小孩一点礼物。

Invite him/her for a meal or give her child a gift.

Situation 7

"不好意思,又让你辛苦了。"

Embarrassing, again let you toil.

"I'm embarrassed to have caused you work hard again."

"辛苦了。"对他人:"他真好"经常抢着做家务。

Toiled. He really nice.

"You have worked hard." Say to other people, "He is really kind." Often look for chances to do housework.

"辛苦了。"

Toiled.

"You have worked hard."

心里感到高兴。

Feel happy from the bottom of my heart.

"嗯,今天你不错嘛。"

Uhm, today you are not bad. "Uhm, you have done well today."

"啊,你做好了,我本来打算回来再做,你真好。"对别人说:"昨天我老公把事情做好了。"

Ah, you done well. I planned to be back to do it, you are really nice. Yesterday my husband get the work finished.

"Ah, you have done it. I was planning to do it when I'm back home. You are so kind." Say to other people, "My husband finished the housework for me."

你辛苦了。"自己尽量找机会多做事。

You toiled.

"You have worked hard." I would find opportunities to do more housework.

补做一些其他事情。

Make it up by doing some other things.

"你帮我做好了。你真好！"

You helped me done. You are really good.

"It was very kind of you to have helped me to finish the work."

"太阳从西边出来了。"

The sun from the west risen.

"The sun rises from the west today."

向他人夸耀对方。

Flaunt about him/her before other people.

玩笑地："表现不错,再接再厉。"

Exhibition not bad, again continue encouragement. Jokingly, "You have behaved well, make persistent efforts."

"不好意思了。"

Embarrassing.

"I feel embarrassed about it."

"谢谢。"

"Thanks."

"你做了我该做的事,不好意思了！该怎么谢你呢？"积极多做家务。

You did I should have done thing, embarrassing. Must how to thank you?

"You have done what I should have done, I feel embarrassed! What should I do to thank you?" Do more housework without having to be asked to.

"太出乎意料了。"

Too out of expectation.

"It was really out of my expectation."

"谢谢你。"以后我会尽量去做。

"Thank you." I would do my best to do housework.

对丈夫的成绩加以肯定,即便他把饭煮坏。

Affirm what my husband has done, even if he has spoiled the meal.

和朋友聊天时讲起。

Talk about it while chatting with my friends.

"你真是我的好老公。"尽力关心他。

"You are really my good husband." Do my best to care for him.

Situation 8

过后，"今天太高兴了，下一次让我请你们一次好吗？"

Today too happy. Next time let me invite you once OK? Afterwards, "I'm very happy today. Next time is on me, OK?"

下次抢着去付钱。

Next time I would vie to make payment.

请对方吃饭或请对方出去玩。

Invite him/her for a meal or invite him/her to go for some entertainment.

心存感激，找机会也请他/她吃饭。

I would remember it and look for a chance to invite him/her for a meal too.

"走，我们去吃冰激凌，我请客。"

Go, we go to eat ice-cream, I invite guests. "Let's go to have some ice-cream, it's on me."

"下回我请你。" Next time I invite you. "Next time is on me."

Situation 9

"太谢谢啦！"

Very Thank.

"Thank you very much."

"您们老人家来看我就行了，不必那么破费。" 经常去看看他们。

You senior guys come and visit me would be good, not necessary that spend money.

"I would feel quite happy that you parents come and visit me, you didn't have to spend that money." Often go and visit them, too.

"怎么带来这么多东西，以后不能这么做了。"

Why brought so much stuff, later cannot so do.

"Why did you bring so much stuff? You shouldn't do it anymore in the future."

"我太有福气了" 送父母亲一些补品。

I very have luck.

"I'm really lucky." Send some tonic food for my parents.

待好父母亲，并用自己的工资给父母买礼物。

I would treat my parents well, and buy some gifts for them with my own salary.

我会感动得流泪的。

I would be moved to tears.

觉得父母太疼我了。

I would feel my parents treat me too well.

以后会好好报答父母!

I would render back to my parents later on.

"啊,带这么多东西来啊!"对别人说:"我爸妈对我真好。"好好孝敬父母。

Oh, brought so much stuff here. My parents treat me really well.

"Oh, you have brought so much stuff for me." To other people, "My parents treat me really well." I would show my filial piety to my parents well.

心里很感激,记在心里,准备报答。

I would feel quite appreciative and keep it in my mind. Be prepared to render it back.

今后报答。

Render it back in the future.

"爹,妈,你们来了?"

"Dad, mom, you are here, eh?"

"给我带来那么多的东西,太幸福了。"

Brought me that much stuff, very luxurious.

"I feel so luxurious that you have brought me so much stuff."

流露出很高兴的样子。

I would show my happy look.

"咋带那么多,不用拿来嘛。"跟别人夸耀这件事。

Why brought that much, don't need to bring.

"Why did you bring so much stuff for me, you really didn't have to do it." I would bring it up before other people.

在平时好好孝敬父母。

I would show my sincere filial piety to my parents in daily life.

对其他人夸耀这件事,让别人羡慕自己。

I would flaunt about it before other people, and enable them to envy me.

"呀,这么多好吃的。"当场拿出来吃。

Alas, so much good to eat.

"Alas, you have brought so much tasty food." Then take it out to eat on the spot.

"不消(不用)这么麻烦了,来看一下就行了。"

No need to be so troublesome, come and visit me is good.

"Don't go to so much trouble, just come and visit me is good for me."

"妈妈,你真好。"用自己的工资给父母买礼物。

"Mom, you are really kind." I would buy my parents some gifts with my own salary.

"谢谢爸爸妈妈。今后不要这样了。我在工作单位还是过得挺好的。"

Thank dad and mom. Future should not be like this. I in work unit live quite well.

"Thank you dad and mom. But you shouldn't do this again in the future. I live quite well in my work unit."

他们走时买些东西让他们带回去。

I would buy some gifts for them to bring back.

今后多孝敬父母。

I would should more filial piety to my parents.

"奥,存心要把我喂成胖子?"

Oh, on purpose want me to be fed to become a fatty? "Oh, are you intending to feed me to be a fatty?"

回去看父母时,也带上他们喜欢和需要的东西。

When I go to visit my parents, I would also bring them some things that they like and need.

"你们带来这么多的东西,咯难拿。"

You brought so much stuff, isn't it difficult to bring.

"It's so difficult for you to bring along so much stuff, isn't it."

Situation 10

"谢谢。"

"Thanks."

"谢谢你。"

"Thank you."

有时说:"谢谢。"

Sometimes I would say, "Thanks." Sometimes I wouldn't say anything.

"麻烦了。"

Troubled.

"I have caused trouble."

Situation 11

"谢谢。"

"Thanks."

"谢谢你。"

"Thank you."

"慢走。" Slowly go "Drive slowly."

"麻烦了,慢走。"

Troubled, slowly go.

"I have caused trouble, drive slowly."

"祝你平安。"

Wish you peaceful. "May you be peaceful."

"麻烦你。"

troubled you.

"I have troubled you."

Situation 12

"不用送了。以后你也来我家玩。"

No need to see off. Later on you also come to my home to play.

"It's not necessary to see me off. Please come to visit my home sometime later on."

"今后来家玩。"邀请朋友经常来家玩。

In the future, come to my home to play.

"Please come and visit my home in the future." Often invite him/her to visit my home.

"今后来我家玩。"

In the future, come to my home to play. "Come and visit my home in the future."

"谢谢你家(您)(你)的款待,下次请你到我家来玩。"找机会回请。

Thank your treat, next time please you come to my home to play.

"Thank you for your hospitality. Next time, please come to visit my home." Find a chance to return the treat.

"谢谢你家(您)(你)了。"

"Thank you."

"哪天有时间来家里闲。"

Which day have time come to home for rest.

"Come to visit my home some day when you are free."

"今天玩得好开心,谢谢你了。"

Today play very happily, thank you.

"We were very well entertained today, thank you."

"多谢了,给你们添麻烦了。"对别人说:"这位朋友家真热情。"朋友到家来时也要一样热情招待。

Many thanks, to you add trouble. This friend's family is truly warm-hearted.

"Many thanks. I have increased your trouble." To others, "This friend of mine is very warm-hearted." I would treat him/her equally warm-heartedly when he/she visits my home.

"不必送了。"

No need to see off.

"You don't need to see me off."

"今天过得真愉快,下一次到我家来做客。"

Today spent really happily. Next time come to my home to be guest.

"It has been very happy today. Please come to visit my home next time."

"太麻烦你家(您)(你)了。"

Too trouble you.

"I have troubled you a lot."

"今天真是太高兴了。"

Today really very happy.

"I am really very happy today."

"不好意思,谢谢。"对别人说:"真不好意思。"

Embarrassing. Thanks. Really embarrassing.

"I feel embarrassed. Thanks." To other people, "I was really embarrassed."

"不用送了,请回吧。"

No need to see off, please be back.

"You don't need to see me off. You'd better go back."

"不用送了,外面冷。"

No need to see off. Outside is cold.

"You don't need to see me off. It's cold outside."

找机会回请。

I would find a chance to return the treat.

"饭菜很可口,吃得很饱。"

Rice and dishes are very delicious. Eaten very full. "The meal is very delicious. I have eaten a lot."

· 150 ·

吃饭时说:"饭菜真香。"送到门口时说:"今天打扰了,改天来我家玩。"

Rice and dishes are really fragrant. Today have interrupted, another day come to my family to play.

Say while eating, "The meal is really tasty." Say while being seen off at the door, "We have interrupted you today. Please visit my home sometime later."

"以后有时间到我家去玩。"

Later on have time come to my home to play. "Please come and visit my home later on."

"谢谢。"

"Thanks."

"不好意思,真的给你家(您)(您)添麻烦了。" Embarrassing. Really have given your family extra trouble. "I'm embarrassed. I have added some trouble for your family."

"太麻烦你了。今天的饭菜真好吃。"

Very troubled you. Today's meal is really good to eat.

"I have given you a lot of trouble. The meal today is really delicious."

对别人说这家人的好话。

I would say something in favor of the family before others.

"谢谢你们的款待,改天又见!"

Thank your hospitality. Another day again see. "Thanks for your hospitality. See you another day."

"谢谢,有机会到我家玩。"

Thanks, have chance come to my home to play. "Thanks. Please visit my home when you are free."

"你进恪(去)得了,我走了。"邀请朋友来家做客。

You go in. I leave.

"You may go back now. I will go." Invite the friend to visit my home later.

Situation 13

"谢谢,真的不好意思"

Thanks, really embarrassing.

"Thanks. I feel quite embarrassed for it."

"不用劳烦(麻烦)了。"

No need to trouble.

"You don't have to trouble to do it for me."

"不用劳烦(麻烦)。"常给老人添饭。
No need to trouble.
"You don't have to trouble to do it for me." Often add rice for my parents.
"让你给我添饭,真的不好意思。"
Let you for me add rice, really embarrassing.
"It's really embarrassing to ask you to add rice for me."
"不好意思。"
Embarrassing.
"I'm embarrassed about it."
"不用了,我自己添。"
No need, I myself add it.
"Not necessary, I will do it myself."
表示不好意思的样子。
I would show my embarrassing look.
要用实际行动回报父母。
I would return the favor to my parents with real action.
很过意不去,绝对不让父母帮自己添。
I would feel quite sorry for that. I would never let my parents to do that for me.
"我自己添吧。"心里十分过意不去。
I myself add.
"Let me do it myself." Or I would feel extremely sorry.
"不用。"并站起来接。
"Not necessary." Then stand up to reach for it.
尽量自己添。
I would try my best to do it myself instead.
"谢谢。"
"Thanks."
很不好意思。
I would feel very embarrassed.
"不用了,还是让我自己来吧。"
No need, or let me myself do it.
"Not necessary, I'd better do it myself."
"谢谢你,妈妈。"
"Thank you, mom."

做个可爱的鬼脸。

I would make a lovely face.

Situation 14

"麻烦您了。我走了,再见。"

Troubled you. I leave, goodbye.

"I have troubled you guys. I'm leaving. Goodbye."

"谢谢您,到此止步吧,我走了,再见!"

Thank you. To here stop. I leave. Goodbye.

"Thank you. You'd better stop here. I'm leaving. Goodbye."

"请回吧。"

"Please go back."

"这次给你们添了不少麻烦,又劳您们到车站送我。如果有机会来(某地名),请事先打电话给我,我来接你们。"

This time have added to you a lot of trouble. Also trouble you to the station to see me off. If have chance to come to (name of a place), please in advance call me, I come to pick you up.

"I have caused a lot of trouble for you. Now you are taking the trouble to see me off to the station. If you have a chance to visit (name of a place), please call me in advance. I can go to pick you up."

"感谢你们的盛情款待。" Thank your warm-hearted treat. "Thank you for you hospitality."

"谢谢你们了,下次我们再见面,请回吧。" Thank you. Next time we again meet. Please be back. "Thank you. See you next time. Please go back."

"谢谢你们了。"

"Thank you."

"多谢了,麻烦你们了。"

Many thanks. Troubled you.

"Many thanks. I have troubled you."

心里感激。

I would feel appreciative in my mind.

"太麻烦你们了,谢谢。"

Too troubled you, thanks.

"I have troubled you too much. Thanks."

表示感谢,并欢迎他们来访。

I would express my appreciation and welcome them to visit us.

"谢谢你！再见！"

"Thank you! Goodbye!"

"我走了。你回去吧，不用送了。"

I leave. You go back. No need to see off.

"I'm leaving. Please go back now. You don't need to see me off."

"谢谢你们对我的工作的配合，也谢谢你们的热情款待。"

Thank you for my work cooperation, and thank your warm treat.

"Thank you for your cooperation for my work. I also thank you for your hospitality."

"非常感谢。"

Very appreciative.

"I feel very much appreciative."

"感谢你们的盛情款待。"回家后，邀请对方到家乡来玩，并以盛情回报之。

Thank your warm treat.

"Thank you for your hospitality." I would invite them to visit my hometown and treat them with the same hospitality.

"非常感谢。"到目的地后，打电话报平安，并再一次表示谢意。

Very appreciative.

"I feel very much appreciative." When I arrive at the destination, I would call to let them know that I'm there safely. Once again, I would express my gratitude.

"谢谢！有机会欢迎来（某地名）玩。"

Thanks. Have chance welcome to (name of a place) to play. "Thanks! Please visit (name of a place) if you have a chance."

"打扰你们这么长时间，不好意思；谢谢你们的盛情款待。"

Interrupted you for such a long time, embarrassing. Thank your hospitality.

"I have interrupted you for such a long time, I feel quite embarrassed. Thank you for your hospitality."

"谢谢，谢谢，再见。"

"Thanks, thanks. Goodbye."

"谢谢，下次再见。"Thanks, next time see you. "Thanks, see you next time."

"谢谢你们这几天来的照顾，以后欢迎到我们那儿玩。"

Thank you for these days look after, in the future welcome to our place to play.

"Thank you for your tendance in these days. You are welcome to visit my hometown in the future."

"再见。"对他人说:"他们接待我接待得真好。"友善地对待每一个人。

Goodbye. They received me treated very well.

"Goodbye." Say to other people, "They treated me very well." I will treat everybody kindly.

CHAPTER 4
TEXT PROCESSING AND LINGUISTIC BARRIERS FOR EFL LITERATURE READERS/LEARNERS

4.1 Introduction

From the traditional approach to the personal-response approaches, and then to the reader-response approaches of teaching literature, there has been a growing concern with the active role of reader in text processing. Obviously, the growth of these modern approaches is like a gust of fresh air that has blown into the suffocating teacher-centered tradition of literature classroom, and has opened up students' boundary of free interpretation, enhanced their motivation in studying literature, and enriched their opportunities for communication with peer students. However, in this general trend of increasing emphasis on the freedom of reader from literary text, there doesn't seem to be enough sympathy for the EFL learners as a whole regarding their specific barriers, especially linguistic barrier that they confront in reading English literature.

This article emphasizes the importance of objective text processing for mature interpretation and as a basis for reasonable subjective responses. Therefore, the EFL teachers are reminded not to forget about the objective part of the text and the linguistic barriers while applying the modern approach, so that pendulum effect will be avoided. This issue will be discussed with support from a minor research project undertaken with a group of Chinese undergraduate students of English major who have been studying English literature as a separate course. Meanwhile, in order to better interpret the barrier, the different understandings of an English poem between a native English speaking couple and two of the Chinese EFL learners will be compared. Finally, with Vygotsky's notion of ZPD, this article will explain the role of teacher and peers in prompting EFL readers/learners in text processing and dealing with linguistic crust effect.

4.2 Roles of Reader in Text Processing

According to the traditional reading model, text processing involves the transmission of meaning from the author to the reader via the text, which serves as a storehouse of knowledge from which information is extracted and passed along unchanged (Straw & Sadowy, 1990). Therefore, students are only encouraged to be passive collectors of data embedded in the text. This traditional model often leads to teacher-centered pedagogy when literature is introduced in TEFL since the students often have to depend on the teacher to check up their interpretations of the text with the standard answers. This has caused the application of literature in language teaching classroom to lose its unique attractiveness.

In the 1980's when the communicative movement began to gather momentum in foreign language teaching, advocates of the use of literature in EFL felt compelled to seek for means of using it communicatively so as to prompt its widespread usage (Hirvela, 1996). What Carter (1988) called "personal-response" approach to literature was seen to have the potential to meet this need. This approach encourages learners to "generate personal responses to something in the text, responses which necessitate the production of original discourse" (Hirvela, 1996). The responses can be highly personal within the author's text, and have thus weakened the authoritative dominance of the teacher in the process of literature teaching. Nevertheless, since they are generally only reactions to the authority of the text, the reading is still considered as a passive interpreting process.

Reader-response theory first originated as a means of literary criticism that challenges traditional emphasis on the author's intention in a text. The basis of this theory lies in the belief that texts exist independent of their authors, and readers take an active role in the creation of meaning. Basically, reading is seen by this theory as a productive activity and readers respond to reader's text instead of author's text. The application of reader-response theory in teaching literature is referred to as "the Reader's Liberation Movement" by Terry Eagleton (1985, cited in Gambel, 1993), since "the reader is liberated from the domination of the text and from the omniscience of the teacher and critic".

The personal-response approach and reader-response approach are both superior to the traditional approach in that they have encouraged teachers to create a student-centered model of teaching literature, and therefore students' opportunities in production of discourse in target language are greatly multiplied. Meanwhile, reader-response approach sounds more advantageous than personal-response approach, because it views reading as a productive activity for readers/learners by responding to reader's text and thus has established the dominant role of reader/ learner in text processing. This notion is especially valuable to be applied in the Chinese context, where literature teaching is traditionally treated as a knowledge- stuffing process. By emphasizing the important and active role of the reader, the teacher will be really encouraged to take on a student-centered teaching model.

In spite of all the advantages of the reader-response approach, there is a hidden tendency that some extremists would go in the process of belittling the importance of understanding literary text as an indispensable step to develop "reader's text". A consideration of the dynamic relationship between real and text world should highlight the need for balance here.

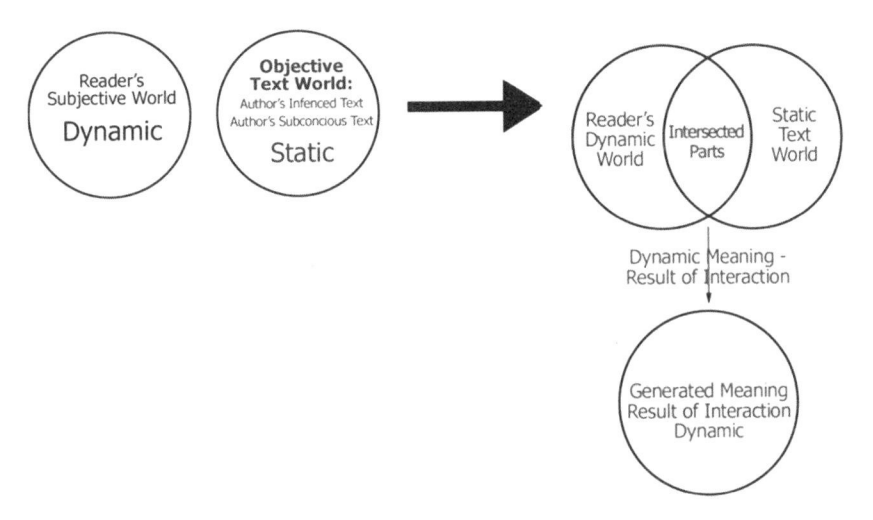

4.3 Generation of Meaning from the Reader's World and Text World

Figure 1 Reader's World and Text World   Figure 2 Generation of Dynamic meaning

I think it is necessary to posit a balanced emphasis on both reader's subjective role and the written text, and that the reader should be regarded neither inferior nor superior to text. The constructed meaning is developed from the intersection between the reader's subjective world and the objective text world. Nevertheless, it is not a mere identity of the intersection, it is a development based on the interaction between the intersected parts of the two worlds. In other words, the generated meaning will no more stay exactly the same as the text was first written; the prior knowledge of the reader can and should be allowed to strongly affect the interpretation. On the other hand, reader's prior knowledge is also activated by and compared with the text, then enriched or adjusted accordingly (refer to figure 1 & figure 2). Spivey (1995) points out that the reader builds meaning from a text by drawing on a number of his/her knowledge sources including rhetorical knowledge, background knowledge and experiences. This is a "constructed meaning" resulted from negotiation between the reader and the text. Beach (1993, 1998) focused on the role of readers' social and cultural knowledge in constructing the meaning of texts, and stated that "readers continually draw on their everyday experience of constructing and interpreting real world contexts to associate certain meanings with certain contexts".

What needs to be specifically pointed out here is that the dynamic nature of the generated meaning originates from the reader's dynamic subjective world and its interaction with the text that vary from person to person and from time to time. The objective text world, which consists of author's intended text and subconscious text, always stays the same, in whatever way it was first written (see Figure 1). Readers never have the authority to make any changes to this static part of the reading activity, which serves as the basis for developing reader's text and should be fully respected.

4.4 Barriers for EFL Readers/learners in Text Processing

During all the interaction between the reader's world and the text world as described above, the richness of the constructed meaning depends on the extent that the two worlds intersect with each other. The more they intersect, the more interaction is to be activated, and thus the more meaning will be obtained. Owing to the various barriers for EFL readers/learners in reading English literature, they often fail to achieve an adequate extent of intersection with the text world to generate a mature meaning from the text.

In Smith's (2000:42-54) account of the EFL readers' barriers to engagement in English literature, she included problems of inappropriate text selection, linguistic challenges, lack of literary competence, cultural barriers, and lack of background information. We will now focus on the students' personal problems and briefly look at each of the relevant issues.

By referring to Smith (2000:46-7), Carter (1986) and Lazar (1993) and in combination with my own understanding, linguistic challenges for EFL readers are generalized as follows:

1. Overload of new vocabulary

A. Dense lexical inventory or neologism to suit special needs in writing

B. Regionalisms, Latinate origins, Lexical mixing

C. General infrequency

2.Ways in which familiar language takes on unfamiliar meanings:

A.Double or multiple word meanings

B.Metaphors and puns

C.Implied meanings of language in the relevant social and cultural contexts

3.Unusual syntactic patterns (especially in poetry)

A.Altered sentence orders and omitted parts of speech

B.Sentence length and related dependencies, embeddings, and subordinations

C.Deliberate suspension or even absence of intersentential cohesion

When Lazar (1993:35) referred to components of background information that might be relevant to the study of specific literary movements, authors and texts, he made the following list, which is outlined here:

1.Biographical information about the author

2.Historical or mythological events or characters to which a text refers

3.Philosophical, religious or political ideas debated in a text

4.Places, objects or other texts referred to in a text-either directly or indirectly

5.Genre of the text

6.Relationship of the text to the literary movements of its time

7.Historical, political or social background against which the text was written

8.Distinct features of the author's style

For cultural aspects, I will just modify the list offered by Lazar (1993:65-66) by pruning out the items that are closely related to linguistic challenges and background information problem so as to best avoid overlapping between the concepts I mention here:

1.Objects or products that exist in one society, but not in another.

2.Social structures, roles and relationships

3.Customs, rituals, traditions, festivals

4.Beliefs, values, superstitions

5.Institutions

6.Taboos

7.Humour

8.Representativeness-to what slice of a culture does a text refer?

The concept for literary competence is a confusing one as it varies from person to person. In order to distinguish literary competence from linguistic competence and cultural and background information, I will generalize it on the basis of Brumfit

(1981:106) as the ability to scrutinize:

1. Interplay of event with event
2. Relationships between characters
3. Ideas and value systems
4. Formal structure in terms of a genre or other literary convention
5. Relationships between any of the above factors and the world outside literature itself

Which of these barriers is the most urgent one of all for more advanced Chinese EFL learners? According to my observation, I would assume that linguistic barrier must be one that stands out. In order to check this hypothesis, I carried out a minor research project.

4.5 Brief Description of Research and Preliminary Discussion

The research project was carried out in two steps. Firstly, a survey was undertaken among 63 junior Chinese undergraduate students of English major. After that, interviews were carried out respectively with two of the students and a couple of native English speakers, seeking insights into the process of literature reading and problems that the EFL learners may come across during the process.

4.5.1 The subjects

In China, children generally begin to learn English from the first year of their junior middle school education. Most urban children even start learning English at primary school. Therefore, by the time they enter their college education, they have already had a history of at least six years of English learning. Owing to the big population and shortage of higher education resources in China, only a small percentage of the children can pass the entrance examinations and go on their schooling in colleges and universities. For those who wish to be enrolled to study English major, they should not only be good in all the subjects so as to reach a bottom line of the total marks, they should also obtain rather high scores in both oral and written English tests.

In the past three years of their college study, the 63 subjects I chose for my survey have been intensively involved in such English skill training courses as comprehensive English, English reading, oral English, composition, and listening course. Therefore, they can be referred to as "elitists" in China regarding their English language competence. English literature is included as one of the English knowledge courses consisting of British literature and American literature, and is taught two hours a week in the last two years of their study at college.

4.5.2 The questionnaire

I composed the questionnaire and attached with it the explanation of each barrier as described in part III in Chinese for the students so as to ensure that the least possible misunderstanding would be caused. The purpose of the questionnaire is to find out their biggest barrier in reading English literature. The students are only requested to make one choice from the four options: insufficient background knowledge, cultural differences, insufficient literary competence and linguistic barrier. The results of this questionnaire are displayed in Figure 1.

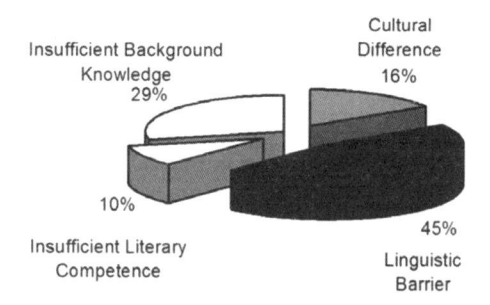

Figure 1 Students perceptions of barriers in reading English literature

The survey shows that 29 students (45%) believed their biggest problem in reading English literature exists in linguistic barrier. This figure is quite in line with the hypothesis I proposed earlier. Let us not to forget yet that these subjects are undergraduate English majors and represent an elite group in the Chinese EFL context. I believe it gives more weight to the implication of this result.

The most striking figure we have obtained from the chart is that only 6 students (10%) claim that insufficient literary competence is their biggest problem when they read English literature.

The explanation for this result is found in my individual interview with one of the students (S1) afterwards who said that literary competence is not a problem for them because it does not change much from one language to another and they have developed this competence largely from Chinese literature reading. He also told me that while they find it very difficult to understand a medieval English novel, they always come across little problem when they read the same English literature in its Chinese Version. Once the linguistic barrier is tackled, all the other barriers would be a lot easier to overcome.

Linguistic barrier is perceived by the a large part of students in this study the most important barrier for EFL learners to deal with in the text processing of English literature, and therefore, must be regarded as significant. For them, there is a hard layer of linguistic barrier to break through so that their reader's world can interact with the text world. Because of this linguistic crust effect, EFL readers/ learners often fail to obtain enough intersection with the text world for satisfactory development of the constructed meaning. Li (1997:7) cites the study of Milton's *Paradise Lost* as an illustration to show students' "linguistic handicap" confronting the teachers of English literature in China, where "almost every line, sometimes every word, has to be explained by the teacher". To EFL readers/learners, the linguistic crust effect takes place also in seemingly simple literary works.

4.5.3 The interviews

The comparison of the responses to Harwood's *In the Park* between two of the students and the two native English speakers as shown below will give us a clear picture of its natures.

In The Park

She sits in the park. Her clothes are out of date.
Two children whine and bicker, tug her skirt.
A third draws aimless patterns in the dirt.
Someone she loved once passes by—too late to feign indifference to that casual nod.
"How nice," et cetera. "Time holds great surprises."
From his neat head unquestionably rises a small balloon... "but for the grace of God..."
They stand awhile in flickering light, rehearsing the children's names and birthdays. "It's so sweet to hear their chatter, watch them grow and thrive," she says to

his departing smile. Then nursing the youngest child, sits staring at her feet.

To the wind she says: "They have eaten me alive"

I, the researcher (Q in the following transcript), first interviewed two of the undergraduate English majors (S1& S2 in the following transcript) with a copy of the poem for each and asked them to read it carefully and talk about it in five minutes. Five minutes later, they carried out the following discussion with me:

Q: Would you tell me how you feel about this poem?

S2: I think this is about a love story. A woman got married with a man and had three children. Then the man had to leave his wife for some reason. The woman waited and waited. One day, she suddenly saw him in the park. She was so excited…

S3: If they were husband and wife, why did the man depart her after that?

S2: Mm… I don't. What does the word "feign" mean?

S3: It means "pretend". The woman tried to pretend an indifferent look to see her former lover. I don't understand who are "they" in "They have eaten me alive"?

S2: Men, I think. She doesn't like men at all.

Q: What does it mean by "but for the grace of God…"?

S2: It means "Thank God. The children are growing up well."

Q: How do you understand "Time hold great surprises"?

S2: I think it means that time keeps all the wonderful things unchanged. But I just don't know why a balloon is mentioned.

S3: The children are playing balloons. The second stanza is not quite important anyway.

The interview with the native English speaking couple was carried out with the same instructions, but they told me that they were ready only after about three minutes' preparation:

NS1: I don't like this poem because the woman sounds quite pessimistic as the mother of the children.

NS2: Pessimistic? I think she was optimistic in spite of all her difficulties. At the end, she said, "They haven't eaten me alive".

NS1: No, "They have eaten me alive".

NS2: Oh, …I'm sorry. Yes, you are right, then. She expressed her feeling of loneliness and frustration by saying that. But I really feel sorry for her to look like that, especially before her former boyfriend. He was obviously in good shape.

NS1: It all depends on how one looks at it. Like Nancy (substituted name), she has four children now, but she is very happy with them. Neither she nor her husband has ever complained.

Q: What does this line mean? "How nice," et cetera.

NS1: By "How nice", et cetera, it just means that they were exchanging some nonsense remarks. It shows here that they did not intend to carry on the conversation to any greater depth, especially the woman. She didn't want him to see the miserable part of her life.

Q: How about "Time holds great surprises."

NS2: No one knows what's going to happen in one's life. Like us, we never expected to live in China twenty years ago. You didn't expect that you would study in Kunming again two years ago, did you? This phrase simply means anything can happen in our life.

Q: What does the expression "but for the grace of God..." imply?

NS2: It was the man's thinking. He felt lucky not to be the husband of the woman and the father of the three children.

NS1: Yes. When we saw a man with broken legs or a beggar, we might say to ourselves, "But for the grace of God, I could have been in the same position." We often omit the second half of the sentence though.

As we compare the above interviews, we can see that the EFL students were unable to give a mature interpretation of the poem mainly because of their incomplete or flawed understanding with expressions like "How nice", "Time holds great surprises", "but for the grace of God..." etc. To native English speakers, however, the implied meanings of these expressions are prompt and natural. The word "balloon", which simply means "thoughts" (metaphor) in the poem, is another example that shows this nature of the linguistic crust effect for the EFL readers/learners.

4.6 More Findings

Several other findings were also obtained from the research concerning text processing and linguistic barriers we discussed above. We will now briefly discuss these issues in the following.

4.6.1 Unavoidable influence of author's text in reading literature

Most readers would follow or seek to follow author's text for reasonable initial interpretation, consciously or subconsciously. Therefore, it seems to be a useless struggle for readers to get rid of author's text altogether. As we can see from my discussion with the two native speakers, they basically agreed with each other once the misreading was cleared up. The reasonable or mature meaning they generated was highly in line with the text that the author intended to convey. In fact, a successful author seldom fails to transfer his/her intended text to the native readers, including information and emotions. Namely, in most cases, readers' consensus lies in the author's text, unless they intentionally denaturalize their reading, whether they are aware of it or not. Therefore, it is not altogether meaningless for EFL literature teachers to deal with the author's text while encouraging them to respond to their reader's text, as long as they do not go to the other extremity.

4.6.2 For EFL readers, "multi-interpretations" or "new ideas" often derive from misinterpretation of the original text

As we have observed from the above conversation, the students seemed to be holding some "new ideas" at first. It was not until I analyzed the conversation into details did I find out that those ideas came from a faulty understanding of the original text. The teacher or the readers/learners themselves could easily neglect such false reading without proper treatment if they are not inquisitive enough or without the guidance of a teacher. Such possibility is increased when students are only encouraged to give their reader response. Many students can still give a great deal of "false response" without really being able to understand the text.

4.6.3 Disguised linguistic barriers are more problematic for EFL readers/ learners than apparent new words

Apparent new words are easy to spot. The students can simply deal with such problems by using dictionaries or asking their teacher or peers as soon as they find them to be in the way. However, they can easily neglect small multi-meaning words, metaphoric usage of words or expressions, unusual expressions that consist of familiar words, or simple expressions that are embedded with rich implications. Meanwhile, teachers, especially native English speaking teachers would also easily ignore these disguised linguistic barriers for their EFL learners because they look so trouble-free. Furthermore, these expressions are generally not regarded as set phrases in dictionaries, enabling them more likely to become blind spots in TEFL context. Therefore, it is the teacher's basic responsibility to identify these hidden linguistic barriers that interfere with their interpretations about the text.

4.7 Vygotsky's Concept of Assistance in Dealing with the Linguistic Barriers and Propelling Intersection

Vygotsky (1978:86) first proposed that there are two children's developmental levels: actual development and potential development. He suggested that there is always a difference between these two forms of development and he named this gap as the "Zone of Proximal Development" (ZPD). "Under adult guidance or in collaboration with more capable peers", children can achieve the level of potential development which they cannot do alone. This notion has been widely appreciated and applied in second language teaching. This concept is also very adaptable in explaining the role of teacher and peers' in assisting EFL literature readers/learners to deal with the linguistic crust effect, and to propel intersection between the reader's world and the text world.

As we mentioned above, EFL readers/learners often fail to intersect their reader's world with the text world sufficiently enough to generate mature interpretation, mainly owing to the linguistic crust effect. However, with the assistance from their literature teacher and/or peers, they are able to gradually fill up the gap of ZPD, achieve the potential level of intersection, and generate a great deal of meaning as a result of an improved intersection between the two worlds (refer to figure 3 over-leaf).

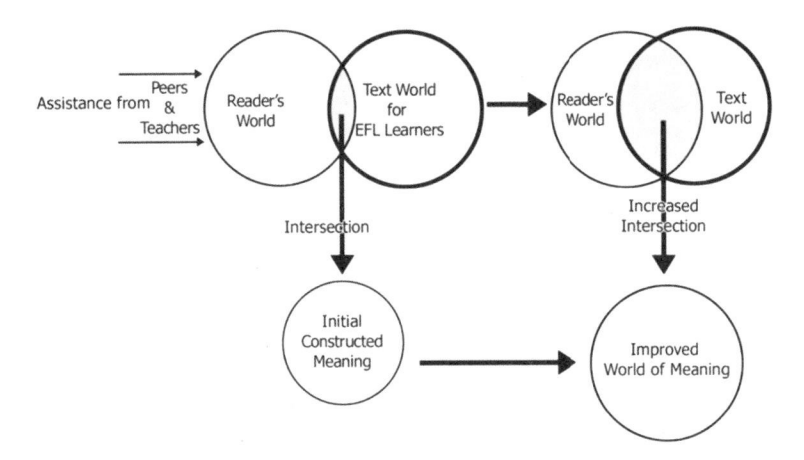

Figure 3   Linguistic Crust Effect and ZPD

Peer assistance, as can be observed from my interview with the two EFL students, should be greatly encouraged in literature teaching owing to its unique advantages. The students helped each other with meaning of words, and they also helped each other with the reasoning process of the story. They both offered each other persistent driving force along the route of telling stories about their own reader's text. As a result of their conversation, they were able to develop a more mature interpretation about the poem. The advantages of peer assistance may be generalized as:

1. Relaxing and friendly atmosphere
2. Student-centered setting
3. Handy aid for lexis
4. Free and prompt modification in understanding text
5. More chances for students to tell about their reader's text
6. More chances to apply their target language in real communication
7. Helpful to build students' self-confidence

However, peer assistance alone is generally not enough for the students to develop ideal and mature responses, as we have noticed in the interview scripts. They often tend to leave their interpretations half way through. Therefore, the role of teacher is of vital importance in furthering students' text processing and thinking along the right track. Basically, while encouraging obscurities and multi- interpretations, the teacher needs to be watchful that these have not originated from flawed or incomplete understanding of the literal text. Before the teacher is sure that the students have comprehended the literal meaning of the text well enough, he/she certainly should not confuse them or reinforce their misinterpretation with denaturalization tasks. Here are a few things that the teacher may do to help the students to overcome the linguistic crust effect:

1. Listen to students' discussion and figure out the problems they may have in understanding the text, then provide relevant explanation.

2. Ask the students questions about certain linguistic items, and find out their problems directly, then provide help if needed.

3. Provide direct teaching of some key words or expressions before students read the text. This is only done when it is absolutely necessary.

4. Provide help only upon request. All the time, the teacher only works as facilitator and keep students motivated in seeking for more accurate understanding of the text and better responses.

Lastly, the teacher can also help them to overcome literary difficulties and text processing quite efficiently by introducing some relevant background knowledge to them or giving them some general ideas about the text.

4.8 Conclusion

This paper has specifically considered the significance of understanding the "objective text" as a basis for good subjective responses to literary texts. Unlike L1 readers, EFL readers/learners generally have to overcome much more difficulties linguistically so that they can generate reasonable meaning through interaction between their reader's world and the text world. This linguistic crust effect was verified in our research. Meanwhile, we find from the study that the influence of the author's text is unavoidable in actual reading; EFL learners/readers often misinterpret the original text and are still able to give active but misled responses; also, disguised linguistic barriers are often easily neglected and thus need to be specifically attended to by the teacher.

In order to overcome the linguistic crust effect, peer assistance as well as teacher's help is needed. Vygotsky's notion of assistance and ZPD can be applied to show how EFL readers/learners can get through the linguistic barriers and achieve an ideal level of intersection between the reader's world and text world.

However, it is necessary to claim here that by dealing with linguistic barriers does not necessarily mean that teachers have to teach literature with the traditional approach. It is just the opposite, by facing the linguistic problem with a realistic attitude will enable us to apply modern approaches in EFL literature teaching more practically and more efficiently.

References:

Beach, R. A teachers' introduction to reader response theories. Urbana, IL: National Council of Teachers of English, 1993.

Beach, R. Constructing real and text worlds in responding to literature. Theory Into Practice, 1998(37/3): 176-184.

Brumfit, C. Reading skills and the study of literature in a foreign language. System, V.9, no.1, 1981.

Carter, R. Simple Text and Reading Text Part 2: Some Categories of Difficulty. In Brumfit, C. & Carter, R. (Ed.), Literature and Language Teaching: 216- 22, Oxford University Press, 1986.

Carter, R. The integration of language and literature in the English curriculum: a narrative on narratives. In S. Holden (ed). Literature and Language. Oxford: Modern English Publications, 1988.

Finegan, E. Besnier, N. Blair, D. Collins, P. Language: Its structure and Use. Harcourt Brace (Australian Edition) Gambell, T., J. 1993. From Experience to Literary Response: Actualizing Readers Through the Response Process. In S.Straw & D. Bogdan (ed). Constructive Reading Beyond Communication. Portsmouth: Boynton & Cook, 1992.

Hirvela, A. Reader-response theory and ELT. ELT Journal, 1996(50/2): 127-134. Oxford University Press.

Lazar. G. Literature and Language Teaching: A Guide for Teachers and Trainers. Cambridge: Cambridge University Press, 1993.

Li, Ming Sheng English Literature teacher in China: Flowers and Thorns. In the Weaver: A Forum for New Ideas in Education, 1997, No.2.

Smith, Erica M. Negotiating Barriers to Engagement with English Literature in EFL Contexts. Unpublished paper, 2000.

Spivey, N. Written descourse: A constructivist perspective. In L. Stoffe (Ed.),

Constructivism in education, 1995:313-329. Hillsdale, NJ:Erlbaum.

Straw, S. & Sadowy, P. Dynamics of communication: Transmission, translation, and interaction in reading comprehension. In D. Bogdan & S. Straw (Eds.), Beyond Communication: Reading Comprehension and Criticism, 1990:21-47. Portsmouth, NH:Boynton & Cook.

Vygotsky L. S. Mind in society: the development of higher psychological process. Edited by Michael Cole, et al. Cambridge:Harvard University Press, 1978.

CHAPTER 5
THE VALUE OF A "WEEKLY ENGLISH DAY"

5.1 Introduction

Chinese English learners were particularly enthusiastic about English Corners a few years ago. But the enthusiasm seems to be dropping dramatically. Instead of a loss of the learners' interest in learning English, the reasons seem rooted in their poor organization. We did not blame our students for not attending English Corners regularly. Instead, we began to try out a well-planned "Weekly English Day", which has proved to be quite attractive to the students.

5.2 Why Do Traditional English Corners Fail?

I have participated in a number of traditional English corners, and I have to admit that I did find them very attractive at the beginning. As time went by, however, I found myself always repeating the same set of questions and answers to whomever I met. Questions like "May I know your name, please?", "Where are you from?", "What's your major?", "How long have you been learning English?", "Do you often come here?" are asked and answered hundreds of times over. Having gone through the usual stereotyped "questions and answers" about various private matters, both sides began to stare into each other's eyes, racking their brains for fresh ideas to continue the conversation. Quite often, the "fresh ideas" were not welcomed by the other side, even disliked by the speaker him/herself, especially when some sensitive private topics were brought up, which usually caused embarrassing awkwardness.

The organization of traditional English corners is doomed to failure, chiefly because of the following factors:

A traditional English corner is usually quite loosely organized and the less committed participants will not attend it if there are other more interesting things to do.

Taking part in a traditional English corner often means being forced to expose personal information to strangers, which can be offensive to many people.

An English corner usually offers participants no theme for discussion and people often feel embarrassed when they cannot come up with anything suitable to talk about.

5.3 How Was the Weekly English Day Started?

I have been teaching the English Listening and Speaking Course for many years. I found that most of my students were fairly eager to take part in the course. However, not much progress was made, although they were all very diligent and sincere. I knew it was because of their lack of using English in real communicative situations. How could they learn a foreign language well through only four hours of listening and speaking a week? I decided to form an English Corner of our own. Unfortunately, it was attended by fewer and fewer students each week, until it was closed down completely a few weeks later. Then, I urged my students to speak English both outside as well as inside the classroom. However, this strategy also lost its effectiveness before long, for the students were not used to speaking English with their classmates after class.

Then I hit upon an idea: Why not organize some kind of interesting group discussion after class? Assuming that my students would be interested if the discussions were organized properly, I set about searching for various types of oral material. However, it was not easy in China to lay hands on any ready-made motivating materials for real discussion, and I had to create our own out of pictures and photos carefully chosen from different books and newspapers. These turned out to be fairly appealing to my students later on. With the memories of the previous unsuccessful English corner in my mind, I knew this idea might also be threatened if our students were given total "freedom" without some discipline. Therefore, I organized the students into groups of four or five members with a group leader they elected among themselves. All students were asked to come to the classroom in time to participate in discussions that were arranged once every week for about two hours each time. For those who did not attend the discussion on time or who did not behave properly, the group leaders were given the authority of reducing some marks from the final scores of the Listening and Speaking Course without the personal knowledge of the offenders. Alternatively, the group leaders could also choose to "punish" them in less harsh ways. As a result, the organized discussions continued smoothly even when I was occasionally absent. Most students really enjoyed the sessions as long as they received a constant supply of fresh and motivating topics from their teacher. It was very inspiring for me to see that the experiment had proved to be quite successful. The idea of the Weekly English Day occurred to me a few days before Children's Day when I was taking a walk after supper. Children's Day is observed once a year on the first day of June, when a lot of activities are organized for children's amusement. I wondered if it would be possible to do the same thing for our students, choosing one day in a week for them to enjoy the pleasure of using English, like enjoying a festival.

Having considered various activities for the day, and the amount of money and equipment needed, I wrote a formal report to the college leaders and asked for their support. Meanwhile, I publicized the idea to my students and colleagues, knowing the importance of winning their cooperation. In face, they all supported the initiative idea enthusiastically, and offered me a considerable number of valuable suggestions, too.

5.4 Activities

In this section, I would like to explain the four main things we do during the Weekly English Day in the following order: an English broadcast; routine communication in English; group discussions; unitizing the video room and language lab; giving prizes to winning editors.

5.4.1 English broadcast

By making use of the college broadcasting station, we have established the "Voice of the Weekly English Day". Instead of running the programs of the day only by teachers or a few best students, we give a chance to all the English major students. They edit as well as broadcast the program themselves in groups with the guidance and assistance from the teachers where necessary. The students were arranged in groups of three or four according to a certain schedule from the beginning of the semester so that they knew long in advance which day they should be responsible for. Thus, all of them are given plenty of time to look out for relevant materials, and plan their program. The students are required to hand in their written plan and recorded tape to the teachers a week earlier for a thorough check before they are actually broadcast. They are then put away as a file for future reference.

5.4.2 Routine communication in English

We have also set up a rule that all the students must speak in English with each other and their teachers both outside as well as inside the classroom on the day. This requirement is much more acceptable to the students than the previous one which simply urged them to speak in English every day. Now they are plunged into the language ocean from the early morning when the English broadcast starts.

5.4.3 Group discussion

Having analyzed the experiences of previous attempts at group discussions, we decided to continue the idea for about one and a half hours in the afternoon with a teacher or two standing by to offer necessary help once in a while. The students are usually high-spirited in their discussion and the activity is often fairly successful.

5.4.4 Utilizing the videoroom and language lab

The establishment of the Weekly English Day helped us to give students more opportunities of listening to all kinds of tapes at the college language lab, and of watching different types of authentic English TV programs received by the college satellite station. Previously these facilities had been under-used. The leaders soon approved the suggestion and allowed students to use the language lab for two hours after the group discussion. They also provided three hours or so in the video room in the evening. This has intensified the language atmosphere of the English Day.

5.4.5 Giving prizes to winning editors

At the end of each semester, all groups of "editors on duty" are evaluated by a special committee comprising the teachers of English. Their work is judged according to the quality of their recorded tapes. As a result, two or three groups of editors are chosen to win the prizes for being "best editor on duty". We have established a few standards to evaluate their work, such as the variety of their programs, the reasonableness and carefulness of the program schedule, the accuracy of language use, and their English pronunciation and intonation. Students are also warned that a group will be chosen as the "Worse Editor-on-duty" so that those with less interest are spurred on to become better.

5.5 How Has the Weekly English Day Turned Out?

It was made clear from the first day that all activities should be arranged mainly by the students themselves with some assistance from the teachers at different levels. This has urged the students to become fully aware of their important position and has increased their motivation.

The editorial work of the programs has particularly interested the students. In the first place, the work is quite challenging and it is not easy to achieve success in the heated competition. Secondly, their imagination and creative ability has found an ideal outlet. Thirdly, they can practice quite a lot of English skills while editing and recording their own programs, such as pronunciation, writing, reading, listening and speaking. They enjoy learning English in such a creative and purposeful way.

Their routine communication in English on the English Day has supplied them with plenty of natural topics for conversation, which is of vital importance in gaining real communicative competence. Through their daily conversations, the are also learning a wide range of words and expressions from each other, some of which may never appear in a textbook despite being rather useful in their everyday life. However, the requirement that they speak English was not that easy to implement at the beginning, though the ultimate aim was for them to gradually get accustomed to using English every day with their fellow students.

The hour or so discussion on their favorite topics is both interesting and effective. Even some quite introvert students find it enjoyable to share different ideas with their classmates.

5.6 Conclusion

To sum up, the organization of the Weekly English Day has proved to be an interesting and efficient means of improving the students' English level, especially their communicative competence. It is hoped that this form of activity could be put into practice in other places with even more successful results.

CHAPTER 6
A RESEARCH ON MONITORING SYSTEM OF ENLLIC ACQUISITION MODEL

By Duan Ping-Hua, Julie Ann Edgeworth, Yang Li-Ping, Shen Zi-La, He Mei, and Hong Xue-Dian

Abstract ENLLIC English Acquisition Model as hypothesized in this paper argues that, firstly, one can not only acquire a language naturally in its native language land, but can also efficiently master it in a non-native language land by creating a natural language acquisition environment combined with the traditional classroom teaching model. However, such an artificial foreign language environment can only be established by enforcing a reasonable monitoring system because of the "native language priority tendency".

A two-year research project was implemented among more than one thousand teachers and students of English major in the English Department of a college, and a multi-interactional monitoring method through the process management of the ENLLIC Oral English course was proved to be necessary, feasible and effective. The research also predicts that an ENLLIC Acquisition Model can be modified and adopted in schools of different levels, so that the English language atmosphere in China and the TEFL efficiency may be improved as a whole.

Key Words TEFL, ENLLIC, acquisition, monitoring and stimulation, language atmosphere

6.1 An Introduction to the Background

6.1.1 Existing TEFL problems in China

According to some previous investigation, about 300 million Chinese, or one fourth of the total population in China, are learning English now. Among them, more than 100 million English learners are students at universities, middle and primary schools. So far, people who have learned less or more English are over 0.4 billion, which is more than the total population of the English speaking countries. However, only less than 20 million Chinese can use English for real communicative purposes, which means that at least 95% of the English learners in China expanded much time, energy and money in learning English but did not achieve substantially. Therefore, for a long time, English education in China was considered as "producing very little effects", "inefficient and time-consuming", "much expenditure but little effect", "high investments but low returns", or "deaf- mute English" by people both in and outside the TEFL field(Li Lanqing, 1999; Jing Shenghua, 1999; He Xiaoli, 2004; Fan Wenfang, 2006; Wang Ping 2006).

6.1.2 Analysis on the reasons resulting in difficult position

The "language acquisition" theory put forward by Krashen (1981) holds that people acquire a language mainly through two ways: one is acquisition and another learning. By acquisition, it means that people acquire a language unconsciously in the practical communicative process with the world. It is a subconscious process and a result of natural communication focusing on meaning, the same way that children acquire their mother tongue. By "learning", it refers to a formal and consciously controlled means of learning a language. Krashen's Monitor Hypothesis points out that people who have mastered a language through "acquisition" can communicate in the language in a relaxed and smooth way; while people who have mastered the language through "learning" would only be able to monitor the language by using its overtly memorized rules, and thus could not use the language freely and fluently in the real communicative situations. Krashen's theories suggest that "acquisition" is more effective than "learning", and the English learners should acquire English in the way like the babies acquiring their native language. Conscious learning only enables the learners to know about the language instead of really mastering the language they have learned. This has been proved by many unsuccessful examples of adults learning English in spite of all their studious efforts, while almost all children have a perfect mastery of their mother language. Children have never been intentionally taught to speak their mother language. Their communicative competence of the language comes from the real communicative situations.

The "Interaction Hypothesis" of Long (1983) put more emphasis on the initiative function of meaningful negotiation in language acquisition. It held that the two-way communication was more favorable to the language acquisition than the one-way communication. In the process of two-way communication, if one does not understand the other, he can indicate it to his communicatee immediately, which would encourage the two parties to conduct meaningful negotiation and modification, and would thus help to enhance the understanding of the language input. Only by the combination of the "comprehensible input" with the "interaction", favorable conditions could be created for the language acquisition (Allright, 1984). The "Output Hypothesis" proposed by Swain (1985, 1993, 1995) also held that although understandable input was the precondition, it was not the ample condition. Only by meaningful language application could the grammatical accuracy of the target language of the learners match that of the native language. The "Output Hypothesis" emphasized that only when the learners were pushed, that is, when they felt that it was really necessary to promote and develop their target language, was it possible for the output of the language to be helpful for the language acquisition.

The above-mentioned theories suggested the important function that the true language communicative environment had on the language acquisition. Although reasons forming the poor achievement of English teaching and learning in China were complicated, despite the factors such as foreign language environment, learning goal, testing model and being eager for instant success and quick profits, the main reason was that the English environment in China was very poor. A lot of people tried every means to learn English abroad. When they came back to China several years later, they still stuttered out their English. The main reason was that there are a great number of Chinese in these English-speaking countries. These overseas Chinese were unable to get into the life circle of the local people because of the differences that existed among cultures and languages. They would naturally get together and speak Chinese. Was there any improvement compared with the English environment in China? It looks as if that for most of the English learners, the better way is to create man-made English language environment in China.

Then, how can we create an English environment that is like one similar to the native English speaking countries in a non-English speaking country like China?

What the TEFL circle explored for a long time were mainly about how to improve the class teaching efficiency, how to manage to realize the principles and methods of communicative teaching to form a certain English application environment in classes. However, because of the limited class time and the large number of students in traditional English class, the practical English communication application assigned to each student was very limited. Then it is very necessary to consider how it is possible to get efficient out-of-class time from the infinite range of demands on students and how to form a typical all-day-round English language environment.

To create a nice English environment out of class, numerous schools organized extracurricular activities such as English corners, English plays, English clubs, English lunches and English festivals (Zhang Xiaowan, 2003; Xue Wenhua, 2004; Wu Hongyun & Hao Caihong, 2006). But it was a great pity that all the attempts to create after-class English environment either were a fine start and a poor finish, or could not form a long-term steady learning form with a decent size because of the limited participants, which could not produce substantial profit that benefited most of the English learners, and therefore it had no great vitality. To create English environment in the non-native language countries seemed like Goldbach's conjecture and terrified the people. For many years, not many people were willing to spend time and energy to conduct further research on it. It certainly has many reasons, and the major one is that the easiest communicative language for people to use is their own native language. In order to guarantee the promptness, integration and naturalness, people would not abandon their mother language, and communicate in a foreign one with the partners who shares the same mother language, unless there is strong internal and/or external impetus. This kind of phenomenon may be called "Native Language Priority", which is a strong inertia that may destroy all painstakingly designed ideal "English paradise" and turn it into an outer form which has undeserved reputation.

The advancing of the conception of establishing English Day was a turning point. On the basis of analyzing the malpractices of the loosely-organized traditional English corners and the reasons why they had weak vitality, this conception pointed out that English Day should be established on the basis of correlated organization forms and good impetus system (Duan Pinghua, 1996). In a short time many places and schools started English Day activities. However, in the practical operating process, many did not set up a good motivating system or did not get strong administrative support, the related activities were finished only on the participants' own initiative. The result was that the English Day became a mere formality and failed to form a steady, large-size, long-term important learning model.

It should be pointed out that the TEFL circle had not paid close attention to the language acquisition process as to how to overcome this "Native Language Priority Tendency", how to make full use of the limitless time outside class, how to create a nice English language environment. There were rare active thought and exploration, either.

6.1.3 The basic ideas and research direction of this study

The English acquisition model of ENLLIC (English-as-a- "Native" -Language Land in China) was build on the basis of the conception of English Day. Its basic ideas were as follows: first, language could be obtained not only by the way of natural acquisition in the native countries, but also by the way of creating a natural acquisition environment on a non-native language land among a certain group of people with limitless time in a certain range of area or with a certain range of time in a limitless space, combining with other language learning methods. The efficiency of this English-acquisition was much higher than that of class-learning alone; second, because of the function of native language priority, this kind of artificial language environment could only be formed by establishing reasonable monitoring and impetus system.

Therefore, the aim of this study project was to smash the trammels of the traditional and unitary class teaching theory, to explore how to set up efficiently a real or close to real English language environment in a country of non-native language like China, finally to form an English acquisition model that perfectly combined the natural acquisition with the means of class teaching. The most difficult thing of this study was to set up a healthy and nice impetus system to control the English environment efficiently in a long term, and continuously gave full play to its important function in English language acquisition. Therefore it was also the focus of this study. In a word, what this study researched on were the necessity, feasibility and effectiveness of establishing a monitoring and impetus system in order to form a long and stable English language environment in a country of non- native language like China.

6.2 Research Methodology and Process

This study adopted a methodology of combining qualitative and quantitative study, conducting ways of survey, interviewing, observing and action researching. It spent 18 months from the March of 2005 to the August of 2006. Participants were all English majored teachers and students of Lijiang Teachers Training College.

The Foreign Language Department of Lijiang Teachers Training College (the former Lijiang Education College) is a big department with more than a thousand students and about 30 English classes. But there are only 43 English teachers who are in charge of the English major teaching and College English teaching, so the tasks are very heavy. The number of students in each class varied from more than 30 to more than 50. Sometimes there are even more than 70 students in one class. Besides, there's a serious shortage of modernized teaching facilities, it has a long way to go to use computers and internet to assist teaching with only 30 computers in the department. Facing the reality of having not enough to go round, to find a way to remedy the serious shortage of teaching facility and to improve effectively the English teaching quality is the common wish of all the teachers and students in the department. Because this study is closely related to the teaching reform and management of the department, it got energetic support from the college's administration. Besides, there are enthusiastic and friendly foreign teachers and overseas students, the students' dorms, classrooms and teaching offices of the Foreign Language Department are relatively centralized in the college, which is easy to assemble all teachers and students to get about. All the above mentioned provided the study project favorable conditions of weather, terrain and human unity.

The implementing process of this study could be divided into four stages: the experimenting stage at all classes (from the beginning of March to April 13 in 2005), unified implementing stage (from April 14 to the end of August in 2005), developing stage (from the September of 2005 to the August of 2006), and perfecting and ripe stage (from the September of 2006 to the January of 2007).

6.2.1 The first stage: the experimenting stage at all classes

This study began on March 1, 2005. A thorough propaganda and mobilization were conducted in the Foreign Language Department. Every class decided its own English Day and began the trial implementation. Each class tried out its own monitoring measures.

Before the end of the first stage, the researchers summed up the feedback on the English Day activities from each class. After each class analyzed its implementation, the Foreign Language Department made a decision that a unified English Day was set up for all the English majored teachers and students, requiring all of them use English as their language for work and life on the whole day of Thursday. Meanwhile, relevant punishment measures were made. The students from the English Service Group were in charge of the monitoring. Then the research work came into the second stage.

6.2.2 The second stage: unified implementing stage

The unified implementing English Day in the whole Department started out on April 14, 2005, a Thursday. All teachers and students signed an agreement with the Foreign Language Department that they would take part in the English Day. The agreement set Thursday as the English Day. In the day, all communication (leaning, eating, working and chatting) among the English majored teachers and students can only be conducted in English. Through the way of signing agreement, the necessity of creating English language environment and setting English Day was further advertised in a larger range. The obligation was clearly stated that English must be used to communicate among the teachers and students on the English Day. Punishment measures were made for violations. Ways to handle the difficult situation caused by English communication were defined, such as looking up in the referece books in advance, going to the third party (including the ENLLIC First-aid Center) for help and asking them the meaning of the words, expressions and sentences that were unknown (at this Chinese or native language was allowed to use), then going on the communication with the partners. If it was needed, body language like gestures could also be used; if it was too difficult to go on the communication, a "translator" could be asked to help the communication. In a word, on the English Day, all the teachers and students should imagine that they live and study in English speaking countries, people around only knew English and they could not speak Chinese or their own native language.

The monitoring model in this stage mainly was: members of the English Service Group brought with them the penalty bag designed and prepared by the department to impose a symbolic fine on those teachers and students who did not communicate in English. Those who were fined could decide how much he/she was willingly to pay and then put the fine into the bag, which was taken as a warning and apology. The little amount of money from the fines was managed by the English Service Group and was used in the students' public welfare.

In order to make convenient for the students checking and using the useful vocabularies in daily communication, lists of everyday expression in both English and Chinese were printed and sent out to every class. In order to promptly solve the knotty problems students met in their English communication, an ENLLIC First-aid Center was set up. Telephone hot line was also installed, and some backboned teachers were arranged on duty in turn all the day round on the English Day.

During the second research stage, the Foreign Language Department held English speech contest and debate contest concerned with the topics of English Day. The purposes of these contests were not only to enliven the campus life and develop the integrated quality of the students, but mainly to encourage students to do further thinking through the speeches and debates in large range of students. The researchers tried to participate in the preliminary and final contests to find out the representative opinions and thoughts of the students, which would provide basis for the next decision-making.

Since beginning of the English Day, students' opinions, suggestions and the improvement of their English communication ability were found out and collected, as well as the working summary of the English Service Group.

The researchers analyzed the problems reflected by the students and made the following conclusion:

1) The form of English Day to create English language environment were welcomed by most of the students, and reflected a very strong mass basis and energetic vitality to a great extent. It could and should be kept going.

2) It was impossible only depending on advocating and one's own initiative to keep on a steady and continuous going of the ENLLIC activities. Effective monitoring and impetus system should be set up to ensure their healthy development.

3) It was rather limited to depend on the monitoring of the English Service Group. A stereo-type, integrated, and multi-category monitoring system should be established to benefit most of the students.

According to the actual situation, the Foreign Language Department made reasonable adjustment on the work of the next step (started from the new school year of September of 2005). It was decided to rescind the way of imposing fine. On the basis of the course of "Oral English" in English major, "ENLLIC Oral English" was set as a required course of the major, using an assessment way of 7:3 (as parts of a whole which was 10) to evaluate the course, which referred to 70% of the students' achievements was consisted of the evaluations from the teachers, students and class basic points. Thus, the course of "ENLLIC Oral English" undertook the monitoring and impetus function of the students in ENLLIC activities, especially English Day activities.

So far, the research work of the ENLLIC English acquisition model of the Foreign Language Department of Lijiang Teachers Training College entered the third stage, which was characteristic of the stereo-type, system and long-term of the monitoring model. It was a developing stage.

6.2.3 The third stage: developing stage

On September 1, 2005, in order to avoid the side-effect brought by the way of imposing fine, as well as to make the ENLLIC activities especially the English Day activities systematize and last long, the Foreign Language Department set up a new course "ENLLIC Oral English" on the basis of the former "Oral English" course. The new course ran through the whole learning process of the students in the college. The key task of the course was to realize the monitoring and impetus on the communication in English among the English majored teachers and students in relevant time (English Day or the Week of English Practice) and in relevant places (ENLLIC Café, etc.).

The course has defined three basic requirements for the students on the English Day of every week: take part in the noon chat or afternoon chat for at least one hour; every class held an English Evening Party for at least one and a half hour; communicate with the other teachers and students in the same department in English. Besides, according to the requirements of the teaching schedule of "ENLLIC Oral English", each student was put into relevant group. Each group was in charge of an one-hour "ENLLIC Oral English" teaching and the organization of at least one English Evening Party.

The new course adopted new implementing plan-assessment method on the "ENLLIC Oral English", using an assessment way of 7:3 (as parts of a whole which was 10), which referred to that students' achievement at normal times took up 70%, while the task exam at the end of the semester accounted for 30%. This fully reflected the procedure management. Forms of task exam at the end of the semester were flexible, such as discussion, debating and explaining. Achievements at normal times were divided into two: individual score and basic class score. Every class was required to conduct the ENLLIC Night activities, well planned and organized. Students organized and presided the activities in turn. The English Service Group evaluated each class on the basis of the attendance and behaviors of every class on the ENLLIC Night, and the whole situation of using English to communicate with others during the day. Students from the same class share the same basic class score. At the class of "ENLLIC Oral English", the teacher was required to bring students' subjective initiative into full play. The students were divided into many small groups, which should organize its own members to finish the assigned teaching task. The teachers would give marks according to the class teaching organization and participating situation. The teachers also gave scores to the noon chat and evening chat according to attendance and students' behavior. Each class had to conduct mutual evaluation at a fixed time, according to their mutual observation and their behavior of using English to communicate on the English Day.

At the end of the third research stage, in order to widely collect opinions, the researchers also collected 28 proposals from the classes. The head-teachers were clearly required beforehand to solicit opinions from all sides by the way of holding class meeting, then edited into a written copy of suggestions. The suggestions showed the following:

1) The noon chat and evening chat had great influence on the students and were effective. Most of the students took part in the chats enthusiastically and positively.

2) Students could not think of fresh and interesting activities to attract others' attention for the English Evening Party since it lasted long. Some of the classes repeated the old games. The evening party appeared lively and the atmosphere nice when the English Service Group came. They thought they could get higher score. Some felt it was dull, some could not learn anything, and some thought it was a waste of time.

3) The English teachers should take part in the noon chat and evening chat more often and set up good examples for the ENLLIC activities.

By synthetical analysis of the above data, the assessment way of the "ENLLIC Oral English" was on the whole effective and feasible for the monitoring and impetus system. It played an important role to improve the practical ability of the students' speaking English. Meanwhile it had positive influence and strong driving force to activate students' self-confidence and interests in learning English. However, it still had rooms to be improved. After the analysis, the researchers proposed to do the following work in the nest stage:

1) In order to make the ENLLIC work systematized and lasted long, to consolidate and develop the present achievements, an ENLLIC Center should be set up, and special person should be appointed to be in charge of the affairs inside the school, and gradually develop businesses outside the school.

2) The actual effect of the English Evening Party should be emphasized, not the formality. That is, the evaluation conducted by the English Service Group should pay more attention to how and whether the activities improve the students' English level and practical ability, they should not evaluate it according to the standards of whether the activities were noisy and how much applause there were in the party. It was not appropriate to use the name of English Evening Party. To avoid the mis-imagination of some of the students, the name could be changed into ENLLIC Night.

3) To ensure the quality of the ENLLIC Night, every class should plan carefully in advance. Different students could organize each night in turn. They should write down the plan and submit to the ENLLIC Center for examination and approval. They could only implement the plan after got approved. The English Service Group should check whether the major contents were carried out according to the original plan. If there were any changes, the class should report the changes to the center at least two days in advance and got approved.

4) All the English majored teachers were required to participated in the noon chat or evening chat, all were offered a free lunch or dinner and a fixed amount of allowance. Their attendance was recorded. Behaviors of the teachers in the ENLLIC activities were routinely evaluated by peers and students. The average score would be calculated at the end of the semester, and was put into the general assessment of the teaching job of the whole semester.

5) Students in the English Service Group should strengthen the day patrol on the

English Day to find out the actual situation of using English after class on the English Day. They should grasp the yardstick of evaluation for every class.

6) Teachers who taught the course of ENLLIC Oral English should make full use of the monitoring and impetus measure of evaluating the achievement at ordinary times, trying to promote the students' sense of communicating in English.

6.2.4 The fourth stage: perfecting and ripe stage

After one year practice, a lot of valuable experiences were summed up, which laid a good foundation for consolidating and improving the implementation of the ENLLIC acquisition model. The course of ENLLIC Oral English was written into "The Teaching Plan of Lijiang Teachers Training College", and was defined as a require course for English major students.

In the early days of the stage (that is the end of September, 2006), the researchers conducted questionare survey and interviews among the freshmen of 2006. There were 146 participants, among whom two were interviewed as random samplings. In the later days of the stage, the former participants were asked to do survey and interviews again, 148 participants did the survey. Four English teachers and 4 of the freshmen were interviewed at random sampling.

6.3 Data Collecting and Analyzing

At the end of the September 2006, the freshmen took part in the survey. 146 questionaires were sent out and all were collected. The following was a comprehensive analysis on the data collected. The specific contents, the number of participants and the answers were seen in Table I.

From Table I we could see that 83.6% thought their greatest pity after learning English for many years was that it was very difficult to communicate with others in English; Only 17.1% and 8.2% of the students chose A. didn't learn grammar well and B. didn't get a high score for exam respectively; Another 6.85% thought there were some other reasons. This showed that students generally thought that their communicative ability in English was very weak after many years of learning English in primary or middle schools, and it also showed the general wishes to improve their ability to use English.

Table I

Table I-Results of the Survey on the Real Situation of the Freshmen

1. What is your greatest regret after learning English for many years?		
A. Didn't learn grammar well	25ps	17.12%
B. Didn't achieve high scores in English exams	12ps	8.22%
C. Still difficult to communicate in English	122ps	83.56%
D. Other reason/s (please be specific)	10ps	6.85%
2. What do you hope to gain as a result of learning English?		
A. Achieve high scores in English exams	1ps	0.70%
B. To freely communicate with others in English	127ps	86.99%
C. To conduct further research about English	25ps	17.12%
D. Understand English in novels and scientific papers	37ps	25.34%
E. Other/s (please be specific)	0ps	0%
3. How satisfied do you feel with your English communication ability?		
A. Very satisfied	3ps	2.05%
B. Satisfied	10ps	6.85%
C. Not satisfied	133ps	91.10%

Remarks: There was no request for choosing only one, some of the students chose two or more, all of which were recorded and calculated.

The answers to the second question also had a clear-cut stand. 87.1% of the students thought that the ideal result of learning English was to communicate freely with others in English; 25.3% chose the result of understanding the original English novels and scientific papers; only 17.1% thought the ideal result was to conduct further research on English and 0.7% the result was to get a high score for exams.

The third question asked the satisfaction degree the students have on their own English communicative ability. 91.1% said they were not very satisfied, 9.6% answered satisfied, and only 2.1% felt very satisfied with their ability. This showed that the students were lack of self-confidence to their English communicative ability at the beginning of entering the college.

After one and a half year of offering the course, that is, after the first survey participants were in the school for three months for three months, another survey was conducted among them. The specific contents and percentage were seen from Table II.

Table II

Table II-Survey on the course of ENLLIC Oral English

1. Among the 70% achievements at ordinary times, which evaluation way has greater influence on creating a nice English Language environment?		
A. Peer evaluation	30ps	21%
B. Mutual evaluation between the students	18ps	12.6%
C. Evaluation from the English Service Group	2ps	1.4%
D. The above three are equally important	92ps	65%
2. How did the course influence your practice of oral English?		
A. Very great	79ps	56%
B. Great	48ps	34%
C. No influence	14ps	10%
3. How did this course influence your interests of Learning English?		
A. Very great	90ps	63.4%
B. No influence	51ps	35.9%
C. Interest became weaker	1ps	0.7%
4. How did you feel about your improvement in speaking English?		
A. Very satisfied	28ps	19.7%
B. Satisfied	75ps	52.8%
C. Not satisfied	39ps	27.5%
5. What improved your English speaking ability?		
A. Dared to speak English	93ps	65.5%
B. A larger vocabulary	16ps	11.3%
C. Enriched knowledge of English	30ps	21%
D. Other reason/s	3ps	2.1%

In order to form a nice English environment, the course of "ENLLIC Oral English" carried the responsibility of monitoring and impetus, and it was realized by the evaluation of the 70% achievements at ordinary times. Question one in Table II was asking the students which evaluation way had the greater influence. 21% of the students thought the peer evaluation had greater influence; 12.6% chose students mutual evaluation and only 1.4% chose the evaluation by the English Service Group. However, 65% thought all three had the same influence, not a single one could be dispensed with. This illustrated that most of the students approved the importance of a stereo-typed, overlapped monitoring and impetus system which benefited both the practical usage of English and improving the whole English Language environment.

The second question was about the degree of the influence on oral English brought by the course. 90% admitted the positive influence on their oral English practice; 56% thought it had greater influence; only 10% thought there was no influence. This showed that most of the students realized the favorable influence brought by the course of ENLLIC Oral English.

The third question was to ask the influence on the interests brought by the course. 63.4% said that their interests of learning English were enhanced, 35.9% thought there were no influences, and only 0.7% thought the interests were weakened.

The fourth question was about the degree of students' satisfaction on the improvement of their ability of using English. 72.5% of the students had positive attitudes; 27.5% felt unsatisfied. This showed that most of the students thought their oral English were improved and raised to a high level.

The fifth question wanted to know the reasons why the students made progress in oral English. 65.5% of the participants thought their speaking ability got improved because they dare speak now; only 11.3% chose vocabularies were enlarged and 21% thought their English knowledge was enriched. This result showed that most of the students dare open mouth and speak English, and realized the harmfulness caused by not dare to speaking English.

The English Day not only drove the students forward, but also produced very good influence on the teachers. Just as one teacher said: the English Day greatly improved our teachers' speaking ability. Taking me as an example, it was very difficult to speak any sentences for there was no environment, and no people you can talk to. Now all teachers gathered together to speak English. You practiced more, you could speak more, then there was no difficulties in speaking English. This was also the views of the most teachers.

Another teacher told the following about the influences brought by English Day:

On the English Day, we young teachers found that we spoke English very smoothly without any stutter. It was very natural and comfortable to speak English. When the English Day began, we thought it would not last long, might be end at most one and half year. It was beyond our imagination that it lasted for two years. It would keep on going, and become better. It could be a miracle.

The research results showed in the following:

1) After three months of setting up the course of "ENLLIC Oral English", most of the students thought the course brought greater influence to them, and they felt satisfied with the improvement in their own speaking English. The interests of learning English were greatly enhanced. These objectively reflected the effectiveness of setting up the course of ENLLIC Oral English and carrying out the relevant activities, which promoted the students' English practical communication ability.

2) As for the monitoring and impetus system, most students thought that the peer evaluation, students' mutual evaluation and the English Service Group evaluation are all important, not a single one of them could be dispensed with. This showed that most of the students understood and support the stereo-type monitoring model implemented by the ENLLIC Oral English course.

3) Most of the students were bold enough to communicate with other teachers and students in English on their own accord after three months learning the ENLLIC Oral English course, realized at the same time that this sense of boldness and initiative brought important and active push.

4) As directors and assistants of the ENLLIC activity, the English teachers were also beneficiaries. Their English language capability can be improved as well by participating in the relevant activities.

6.4 Limitations of This Study and Suggestions for Further Research

1. The presider of the study project is also the right person in charge of the Foreign Language Department. Although he provided very good administrative support to the smooth conducting of the study, he was still limited by choosing what kind of experimental method, as for one of his study purposes was to improve the English language proficiency of all teachers and students in the department. From his point of

view, there were definitely more advantages than disadvantages for the students to conduct the ENLLIC English acquisition model. He would not want to see that some of the students benifited from it while some did not because the later ones could not take part in the activities. Influenced by the idea, there were no experimental group or comparing group from the beginning of the study.

As a result, the researchers could not use the comparing methodology to test the effectiveness of the study, which was a great imperfection. Therefore, appropriate time and place should be chosen for further research.

2. The monitoring and impetus system and its data analysis were centered around the English Day. Other formalities of ENLLIC English acquisition model were successfully conducted during the process of this study, such as English Practice Week, ENLLIC Cafe, and ENLLIC First-aid Center, and ENLLIC Summer Camp which faced the middle and primary schools. However, this research report did not involve the relevant data, analysis and results, which could be completed gradually in the next research.

3. The study was limited to the English major in only one college. It has great values and potential to be recommended to various kinds of schools for further research.

4. The conception of ENLLIC English Acquisition Model may be applied to teaching Chinese to foreign students or other foreign languages teaching, which needed further exploration.

6.5 Conclusion

From the above analysis, we could draw conclusions that it is necessary, feasible and effective to set up a stable and long-lasted English language environment in a non-native language country like China. The ENLLIC English Acquisition Model, especially the assessment method of the ENLLIC Oral English course, experimented by the Foreign Language Department of Lijiang Teachers Training College, obviously brought more advantages than disadvantages to the English majored students in a non-native environment. After one year learning the ENLLIC Oral English course, most of the students overcame the difficulties that it was hard to open mouth and speak English. They speak more English than before. Their interests and self-confidence in learning English were enhanced, and their ability of speaking English was greatly improved. This study further confirmed the decisive function of an effective monitoring and evaluation system in setting up a real or close-to-real English language application environment in a non-native English environment. It also demonstrated that the key of whether the monitoring system could take into play lied at the specific implementing process of the monitoring and impetus system.

It was predicted by this study that if middle, primary and other colleges and universities are recommended to do popularized researches on the ENLLIC English Acquisition Model, the phenomenon of "more expenditure but less effect" and "deaf-mute English" in TESL of China will be completely changed.

References:

Allright, R. The importance of interaction in classroom language learning [J]. Applied Linguistics 5, 1984.

Krashen, S. Second Language Acquisition and Second Language Learning [M]. Oxford: Pergamon, 1981.

Krashen, S. Principles and practice in Second Language Acquisition [M]. London: Longman, 1982.

Long, M. H. Native speaker/non-native speaker conversation in the second language classroom [A]. In M. Clarke & J. Handscombe (eds.). On TESOL' 82: Pacific Perspectives on Language Learning and Teaching [C]. Washington, D.C.: TESOL, 1983.

Swain, M. Communicative competence: Some roles of comprehensible input and comprehensible output in its development [A]. In S. Gass & C. Madden (eds.). Input in Second Language Acquisition [C]. Rowley, Mass.: Newbury House, 1985.

Swain, M. The output hypothesis: just speaking and writing aren't enough [J]. The Canadian Modern Language Review 50, 1993.

Swain, M. Three functions of output in second language learning [A]. In G. Cook & B. Seidlehofer (eds.). For H. G. Widdowson: Principles and Practice in the Study of Language [C]. Oxford: Oxford University Press, 1995.

段平华. (1996). The Value of a Weekly English Day. 中国英语教学, 1996 (28):40-42.

李岚清.李岚清副总理关于外语教学改革的讲话.文汇报, 1999-09-03。

范文芳.大、中、小学英语教学的"一条龙"规则.外语教学与研究(外国语双月刊),2000(6):442.

何筱莉.浅论英语教学中的"极化"现象.亳州师范高等专科学校学报,2004(6):76-79.

井升华.我国大学英语教学费时低效的原因.外语教学与研究,1999(4):21.

王萍.低效外语教学的成因分析.中国基础教育网,2006.

吴红云,郝彩虹.英语学习需要建构的语言环境.光明日报,2006-08-2.

新华社.专家称我国学英语者将超过英语母语国家总人口.www.chinajilin.com.cn,2006-3-27.

徐文晔.办出特色 促进学校发展.上海师资培训通讯,2004(1):17.

张正东."对外语教学的五点看法".中小学外语教学,2000(2).

张小皖.第二语言习得理论在小学英语教学中的运用.上海师资培训通讯,2003(3):12-13.